M000250247

Introduction to Logic

MASTER BOOKS
CURRICULUM

Master Books Creative Team:
Author: Jason Lisle
Editor: Craig Froman
Design: Terry White
Cover Design: Diana Bogardus
Copy Editors: Judy Lewis, Willow Meek
Curriculum Review: Kristin Pratt, Laura Welch, Diana Bogardus

First printing: December 2018
Fourth printing: August 2020

Master Books® is a division of the New Leaf Publishing Group, Inc.

ISBN: 978-1-68344-149-6
ISBN: 978-1-61458-697-5 (digital)

Unless otherwise noted, Scripture quotations are from the New King James Version of the Bible.

Printed in the United States of America

Please visit our website for other great titles:
www.masterbooks.com

Dr. Jason Lisle is a Christian astrophysicist who writes and speaks on various topics relating to science and the defense of the Christian faith. He graduated from Ohio Wesleyan University where he majored in physics and astronomy and minored in mathematics. He then earned a master's degree and a Ph.D. in astrophysics at the University of Colorado in Boulder. His well-known book, *The Ultimate Proof of Creation*, demonstrates that biblical creation is the only logical possibility for origins. Dr. Lisle currently heads up the *Biblical Science Institute*.

Affordable
Flexible
Faith Building

Table of Contents

Using This Teacher Guide

Features: The suggested weekly schedule enclosed has easy-to-manage lessons that guide the reading, worksheets, and all assessments. The pages of this guide are perforated and three-hole punched so materials are easy to tear out, hand out, grade, and store. Teachers are encouraged to adjust the schedule and materials needed in order to best work within their unique educational program.

Lesson Scheduling: Students are instructed to read the pages in their book and then complete the corresponding section provided by the teacher. Assessments that may include worksheets, activities, quizzes, and tests are given at regular intervals with space to record each grade. Space is provided on the weekly schedule for assignment dates, and flexibility in scheduling is encouraged. Teachers may adapt the scheduled days per each unique student situation. As the student completes each assignment, this can be marked with an "X" in the box.

	Approximately 30 to 45 minutes per lesson, five days a week
	Includes answer keys for worksheets, quizzes, and tests.
	Worksheets for each reading portion
	Quizzes and tests are included to help reinforce learning and provide assessment opportunities.
	Designed for grades 8 to 10 in a one-year course to earn 1 elective credit

Course Description

Welcome to the world of logic. This logic course will both challenge and inspire high school students to be able to defend their faith against atheists and skeptics alike.

Because learning logical terms and principles is often like learning a foreign language, the course has been developed to help students of logic learn the practical understanding of logical arguments. To make the course content easier to grasp, the schedule provides worksheets and practice sheets to help students better recognize logical fallacies, as well as review weeks for the quizzes and the final. The practice sheets in the back of the book offer practical study for both the final exam and for actual arguments you might encounter online or in the media. The practice sheets used in review before the end of the course come from all of the chapters and help students prepare for the final exam.

Memorization Cards: Another way to help understand and memorize new terms is by creating flash cards or memorization cards. It should be noted that this is a part of nearly every week of study on the schedule provided. As new concepts are added each week, it is suggested that this review time grow to allow review of older concepts and the addition of the new terms. Students can make their own flashcards on 3 x 5 cards (the term on one side and the definition on the other), or they might find a flashcard app that can be used from a phone or computer.

To think logically is to think — in a sense — like God thinks. So, by studying logic, you are actually studying theology! This is a great point to emphasize for students who fancy themselves theologians, but are not terribly excited about logic. Students planning on going into ministry better learn something about the mind of the God they serve. Students of science better learn something about God's mind since it is God's mind that controls every atom in the universe. Knowing how their Creator thinks will give them an edge over secular students. Emphasize how awesome it is that we are learning about God's mind! It would be wonderful to learn how Leonardo da Vinci's mind worked, or Albert Einstein's. How much more awesome to learn about the mind of God!

Studies have shown that students learn far more effectively and retain information better if they are exposed to it in short bursts over a long period of time rather than in a long burst of short duration. The student who studies a topic for 40 hours in one week will not retain it nearly as well in long-term memory as a student who studies for a total of 40 hours spread out over two months. For this reason, it is helpful to occasionally ask the student to recall information learned in previous chapters. This reinforces the topic, helps with memorization, and may help the student to think about the older material in light of the newer material. For these reasons and more, we stop and review fallacies covered in previous chapters.

NOTE: In the answer keys Dr. Lisle sometimes adds explanation to the answers that will help the teacher, but this is not required for the student to know for their answers.

First Semester Suggested Daily Schedule

Date	Day	Assignment	Due Date	✓	Grade
		First Semester-First Quarter			
Week 1	Day 1	Read Ch. 1: Logic and the Christian Worldview Pages 5-6 • *Introduction to Logic* • (ITL)			
	Day 2	Read Ch. 1: Logic and the Christian Worldview Pages 7-8 • (ITL)			
	Day 3	Complete Worksheet 1 • Questions 1-5 • Pages 17-18 *Teacher Guide* • (TG)			
	Day 4	Complete Worksheet 1 • Questions 6-10 • Page 18 • (TG)			
	Day 5	Begin Creating Memorization Cards • Review Key Terms			
Week 2	Day 6	Read Ch. 2: All Knowledge Is Ultimately from God Pages 9-10 • (ITL)			
	Day 7	Read Ch. 2: All Knowledge Is Ultimately from God Pages 11-12 • (ITL)			
	Day 8	Complete Worksheet 2 • Questions 1-5 • Pages 19-20 • (TG)			
	Day 9	Complete Worksheet 2 • Questions 6-10 • Page 20 • (TG)			
	Day 10	Continue Creating Memorization Cards • Review Key Terms			
Week 3	Day 11	Read Ch. 3: Why Study Logic? • Pages 13-15 • (ITL)			
	Day 12	Read Ch. 3: Why Study Logic? • Pages 16-18 • (ITL)			
	Day 13	Complete Worksheet 3 • Questions 1-5 • Pages 21-22 • (TG)			
	Day 14	Complete Worksheet 3 • Questions 6-10 • Page 22 • (TG)			
	Day 15	Continue Creating Memorization Cards • Review Key Terms			
Week 4	Day 16	Read Ch. 4: Propositions and Arguments • Pages 19-20 • (ITL)			
	Day 17	Read Ch. 4: Propositions and Arguments • Pages 21-22 • (ITL)			
	Day 18	Complete Worksheet 4 • Questions 1-13 • Pages 23-24 • (TG)			
	Day 19	Complete Worksheet 4 • Questions 14-18 • Page 24 • (TG)			
	Day 20	Continue Creating Memorization Cards • Review Key Terms			
Week 5	Day 21	Read Ch. 5: Inductive and Deductive Reasoning Pages 23-25 • (ITL)			
	Day 22	Complete Worksheet 5 • Questions 1-14 • Pages 25-26 • (TG)			
	Day 23	Read Ch. 6: The Biblical Basis for the Laws of Logic Pages 27-32 • (ITL)			
	Day 24	Complete Worksheet 6 • Questions 1-12 • Pages 27-28 • (TG)			
	Day 25	Continue Creating Memorization Cards • Review Key Terms			
Week 6	Day 26	Read Ch. 7: Logical Failure of the Unbiblical Worldview Pages 33-35 • (ITL)			
	Day 27	Read Ch. 7: Logical Failure of the Unbiblical Worldview Pages 36-38 • (ITL)			
	Day 28	Complete Worksheet 7 • Questions 1-5 • Page 29 • (TG)			
	Day 29	Complete Worksheet 7 • Questions 6-10 • Page 30 • (TG)			
	Day 30	Continue Creating Memorization Cards • Review Key Terms			

Date	Day	Assignment	Due Date	✓	Grade
Week 7	Day 31	Read Ch. 8: Is the Christian Faith Illogical? • Pages 39-40 • (ITL)			
	Day 32	Read Ch. 8: Is the Christian Faith Illogical? • Pages 41-42 • (ITL)			
	Day 33	Complete Worksheet 8 • Questions 1-3 • Page 31 • (TG)			
	Day 34	Complete Worksheet 8 • Questions 4-6 • Page 32 • (TG)			
	Day 35	Continue Creating Memorization Cards • Review Key Terms			
Week 8	Day 36	Read Ch. 9: Is Faith Contrary to Reason? • Pages 43-45 • (ITL)			
	Day 37	Read Ch. 9: Is Faith Contrary to Reason? • Pages 46-48 • (ITL)			
	Day 38	Complete Worksheet 9 • Questions 1-5 • Pages 33-34 • (TG)			
	Day 39	Complete Worksheet 9 • Questions 6-9 • Page 34 • (TG)			
	Day 40	Continue Creating Memorization Cards • Review Key Terms			
Week 9	Day 41	Review Worksheets 1-3 • (TG)			
	Day 42	Review Worksheets 4-6 • (TG)			
	Day 43	Review Worksheets 7-9 • (TG)			
	Day 44	**Take Quiz 1** • Page 115 • (TG)			
	Day 45	Review Key Terms			
First Semester-Second Quarter					
Week 1	Day 46	Read Ch. 10: Arbitrariness and Inconsistency • Pages 49-51 • (ITL)			
	Day 47	Read Ch. 10: Arbitrariness and Inconsistency • Pages 52-53 • (ITL)			
	Day 48	Complete Worksheet 10 • Questions 1-5 • Pages 35-36 • (TG)			
	Day 49	Complete Worksheet 10 • Questions 6-10 • Page 36 • (TG)			
	Day 50	Continue Creating Memorization Cards • Review Key Terms			
Week 2	Day 51	Read Ch. 11: Definitions • Pages 55-57 • (ITL)			
	Day 52	Read Ch. 11: Definitions • Pages 58-60 • (ITL)			
	Day 53	Read Ch. 11: Definitions • Pages 61-64 • (ITL)			
	Day 54	Complete Worksheet 11 • Questions 1-6 • Pages 37-38 • (TG)			
	Day 55	Continue Creating Memorization Cards • Review Key Terms			
Week 3	Day 56	Read Ch. 12: A Brief Introduction to Syllogisms Pages 65-68 • (ITL)			
	Day 57	Complete Worksheet 12 • Questions 1-10 • Pages 39-40 • (TG)			
	Day 58	Read Ch. 13: Enthymemes • Pages 69-74 • (ITL)			
	Day 59	Complete Worksheet 13 • Questions 1-10 • Pages 41-42 • (TG)			
	Day 60	Continue Creating Memorization Cards • Review Key Terms			
Week 4	Day 61	Read Ch. 14: Informal Logical Fallacies • Pages 75-76 • (ITL)			
	Day 62	Read Ch. 14: Informal Logical Fallacies • Pages 77-78 • (ITL)			
	Day 63	Complete Worksheet 14 • Questions 1-4 • Pages 43-44 • (TG)			
	Day 64	Complete Worksheet 14 • Questions 5-8 • Page 44 • (TG)			
	Day 65	Continue Creating Memorization Cards • Review Key Terms			

Date	Day	Assignment	Due Date	✓	Grade
Week 5	Day 66	Review Worksheets 10-11 • (TG)			
	Day 67	Review Worksheets 12-13 • (TG)			
	Day 68	Review Worksheet 14 • (TG)			
	Day 69	**Take Quiz 2** • Pages 117-118 • (TG)			
	Day 70	Review Key Terms			
Week 6	Day 71	Read Ch. 15: Equivocation • Pages 79-80 • (ITL)			
	Day 72	Read Ch. 15: Equivocation • Pages 81-82 • (ITL)			
	Day 73	Complete Worksheet 15 • Questions 1-5 • Pages 45-46 • (TG)			
	Day 74	Complete Worksheet 15 • Questions 6-10 • Page 46 • (TG)			
	Day 75	Continue Creating Memorization Cards • Review Key Terms			
Week 7	Day 76	Read Ch. 16: Reification • Pages 83-84 • (ITL)			
	Day 77	Read Ch. 16: Reification • Pages 85-86 • (ITL)			
	Day 78	Complete Worksheet 16 • Questions 1-5 • Pages 47-48 • (TG)			
	Day 79	Complete Worksheet 16 • Questions 6-10 • Page 48 • (TG)			
	Day 80	Continue Creating Memorization Cards • Review Key Terms			
Week 8	Day 81	Read Ch. 17: The Fallacy of Accent • Pages 87-88 • (ITL)			
	Day 82	Complete Worksheet 17 • Questions 1-10 • Pages 49-50 • (TG)			
	Day 83	Read Ch. 18: The Fallacies of Composition and Division Pages 89-92 • (ITL)			
	Day 84	Complete Worksheet 18 • Questions 1-10 • Pages 51-52 • (TG)			
	Day 85	Continue Creating Memorization Cards • Review Key Terms			
Week 9	Day 86	Read Ch. 19: Hasty Generalization and Sweeping Generalization Pages 93-95 • (ITL)			
	Day 87	Read Ch. 19: Hasty Generalization and Sweeping Generalization Read Pages 96-97 • (ITL)			
	Day 88	Complete Worksheet 19 • Questions 1-5 • Pages 53-54 • (TG)			
	Day 89	Complete Worksheet 19 • Questions 6-10 • Page 54 • (TG)			
	Day 90	Continue Creating Memorization Cards • Review Key Terms			
		Mid-Term Grade			

Second Semester Suggested Daily Schedule

Date	Day	Assignment	Due Date	✓	Grade
		Second Semester-Third Quarter			
Week 1	Day 91	Review Worksheets 15-16 • (TG)			
	Day 92	Review Worksheets 17-18 • (TG)			
	Day 93	Review Worksheet 19 • (TG)			
	Day 94	**Take Quiz 3** • Pages 119-120 • (TG)			
	Day 95	Review Key Terms			
Week 2	Day 96	Read Ch. 20: The Fallacy of False Cause • Pages 99-100 • (ITL)			
	Day 97	Read Ch. 20: The Fallacy of False Cause • Pages 101-103 • (ITL)			
	Day 98	Complete Worksheet 20 • Questions 1-5 • Pages 55-56 • (TG)			
	Day 99	Complete Worksheet 20 • Questions 6-10 • Page 56 • (TG)			
	Day 100	Continue Creating Memorization Cards • Review Key Terms			
Week 3	Day 101	Read Ch. 21: Begging the Question • Pages 105-106 • (ITL)			
	Day 102	Read Ch. 21: Begging the Question • Pages 107-109 • (ITL)			
	Day 103	Complete Worksheet 21 • Questions 1-5 • Pages 57-58 • (TG)			
	Day 104	Complete Worksheet 21 • Questions 6-10 • Page 58 • (TG)			
	Day 105	Continue Creating Memorization Cards • Review Key Terms			
Week 4	Day 106	Read Ch. 22: Begging the Question — Part 2 Pages 111-114 • (ITL)			
	Day 107	Complete Worksheet 22 • Questions 1-10 • Pages 59-60 • (TG)			
	Day 108	Read Ch. 23: The Question-Begging Epithet Pages 115-118 • (ITL)			
	Day 109	Complete Worksheet 23 • Questions 1-10 • Pages 61-62 • (TG)			
	Day 110	Continue Creating Memorization Cards • Review Key Terms			
Week 5	Day 111	Read Ch. 24: The Complex Question • Pages 119-122 • (ITL)			
	Day 112	Complete Worksheet 24 • Questions 1-10 • Pages 63-64 • (TG)			
	Day 113	Read Ch. 25: The Bifurcation Fallacy • Pages 123-126 • (ITL)			
	Day 114	Complete Worksheet 25 • Questions 1-10 • Pages 65-66 • (TG)			
	Day 115	Continue Creating Memorization Cards • Review Key Terms			
Week 6	Day 116	Read Ch. 26: The No True Scotsman Fallacy Pages 127-128 • (ITL)			
	Day 117	Complete Worksheet 26 • Questions 1-10 • Pages 67-68 • (TG)			
	Day 118	Read Ch. 27: Special Pleading • Pages 129-132 • (ITL)			
	Day 119	Complete Worksheet 27 • Questions 1-10 • Pages 69-70 • (TG)			
	Day 120	Continue Creating Memorization Cards • Review Key Terms			
Week 7	Day 121	Read Ch. 28: The False Analogy and the Slippery Slope Fallacy Pages 133-135 • (ITL)			
	Day 122	Complete Worksheet 28 • Questions 1-10 • Pages 71-72 • (TG)			
	Day 123	Read Ch. 29: Review of the Fallacies of Presumption Pages 137-139 • (ITL)			
	Day 124	Complete Worksheet 29 • Questions 1-10 • Pages 73-74 • (TG)			
	Day 125	Continue Creating Memorization Cards • Review Key Terms			

Date	Day	Assignment	Due Date	✓	Grade
	Day 126	Read Ch. 30: *Ad Hominem* • Pages 141-142 • (ITL)			
	Day 127	Read Ch. 30: *Ad Hominem* • Page 143 • (ITL)			
Week 8	Day 128	Complete Worksheet 30 • Questions 1-5 • Pages 75-76 • (TG)			
	Day 129	Complete Worksheet 30 • Questions 6-10 • Page 76 • (TG)			
	Day 130	Continue Creating Memorization Cards • Review Key Terms			
	Day 131	Review Worksheets 20-23 • (TG)			
	Day 132	Review Worksheets 24-27 • (TG)			
Week 9	Day 133	Review Worksheets 28-30 • (TG)			
	Day 134	**Take Quiz 4** • Pages 121-122 • (TG)			
	Day 135	Review Key Terms			
Second Semester-Fourth Quarter					
	Day 136	Read Ch. 31: The Faulty Appeal to Authority Pages 145-146 • (ITL)			
	Day 137	Read Ch. 31: The Faulty Appeal to Authority Read Pages 147-149 • (ITL)			
Week 1	Day 138	Complete Worksheet 31 • Questions 1-5 • Pages 77-78 • (TG)			
	Day 139	Complete Worksheet 31 • Questions 6-10 • Page 78 • (TG)			
	Day 140	Continue Creating Memorization Cards • Review Key Terms			
	Day 141	Read Ch. 32: The Strawman Fallacy • Pages 151-152 • (ITL)			
	Day 142	Read Ch. 32: The Strawman Fallacy • Page 153 • (ITL)			
Week 2	Day 143	Complete Worksheet 32 • Questions 1-3 • Pages 79-80 • (TG)			
	Day 144	Complete Worksheet 32 • Questions 4-5 • Page 80 • (TG)			
	Day 145	Continue Creating Memorization Cards • Review Key Terms			
	Day 146	Read Ch. 33: Faulty Appeals • Pages 155-156 • (ITL)			
	Day 147	Read Ch. 33: Faulty Appeals • Page 157 • (ITL)			
Week 3	Day 148	Complete Worksheet 33 • Questions 1-5 • Page 81 • (TG)			
	Day 149	Complete Worksheet 33 • Questions 6-10 • Page 82 • (TG)			
	Day 150	Continue Creating Memorization Cards • Review Key Terms			
	Day 151	Read Ch. 34: Naturalistic, Moralistic, and the Appeal to Consequences • Pages 159-160 • (ITL)			
	Day 152	Read Ch. 34: Naturalistic, Moralistic, and the Appeal to Consequences • Page 161 • (ITL)			
Week 4	Day 153	Complete Worksheet 34 • Questions 1-5 • Pages 83-84 • (TG)			
	Day 154	Complete Worksheet 34 • Questions 6-10 • Page 84 • (TG)			
	Day 155	Continue Creating Memorization Cards • Review Key Terms			
	Day 156	Read Ch. 35: The Genetic Fallacy and the Tu Quoque Fallacy Pages 163-164 • (ITL)			
	Day 157	Read Ch. 35: The Genetic Fallacy and the Tu Quoque Fallacy Page 165 • (ITL)			
Week 5	Day 158	Complete Worksheet 35 • Questions 1-4 • Page 85 • (TG)			
	Day 159	Complete Worksheet 35 • Questions 5-8 • Page 86 • (TG)			
	Day 160	Continue Creating Memorization Cards • Review Key Terms			

Date	Day	Assignment	Due Date	✓	Grade
Week 6	Day 161	Read Ch. 36: The Fallacy of Irrelevant Thesis Pages 167-168 • (ITL)			
	Day 162	Complete Worksheet 36 • Questions 1-10 • Pages 87-88 • (TG)			
	Day 163	Read Ch. 37: Review of Fallacies of Relevance Pages 169-171 • (ITL)			
	Day 164	Complete Worksheet 37 • Questions 1-10 • Pages 89-90 • (TG)			
	Day 165	Continue Creating Memorization Cards • Review Key Terms			
Week 7	Day 166	Read Ch. 38: Closing Remarks • Page 173 • (ITL)			
	Day 167	Read Ch. 38: Closing Remarks • Page 174 • (ITL)			
	Day 168	Finish Creating Memorization Cards • Review Key Terms			
	Day 169	Review Worksheets 31-33 • (TG)			
	Day 170	Review Worksheets 34-36 • (TG)			
Week 8	Day 171	Review Worksheet 37 • (TG)			
	Day 172	**Take Quiz 5** • Pages 123-124 • (TG)			
	Day 173	Complete Practice Sheet 1 • Page 93 • (TG)			
	Day 174	Complete Practice Sheet 2 • Page 95 • (TG)			
	Day 175	Complete Practice Sheet 3 • Page 97 • (TG)			
Week 9	Day 176	Complete Practice Sheet 4 • Page 99 • (TG)			
	Day 177	Complete Practice Sheets 5-6 • Pages 101 and 103 • (TG)			
	Day 178	Complete Practice Sheets 7-8 • Pages 105 and 107 • (TG)			
	Day 179	Complete Practice Sheets 9-10 • Pages 109 and 111 • (TG)			
	Day 180	**Take Final Exam** • Pages 125-126 • (TG)			
		Final Grade			

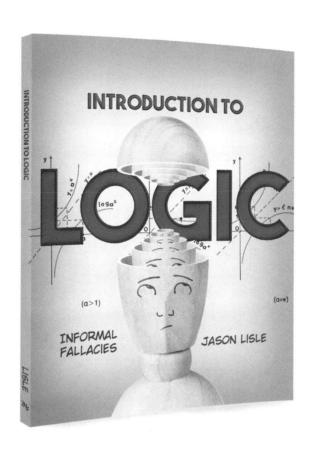

Logic Worksheets

for Use with

Introduction to Logic

Chapter Review: The goal of this chapter is to explore the Christian basis for logic. We define what logic is and clarify misconceptions about what logic is not. Then we see how logic is rooted in the mind of God. Logic is not a neutral topic. It is distinctly Christian. Anyone who uses logic therefore demonstrates that the Christian worldview is true, even if the person himself professes to reject Christianity. Key points in this chapter are:

  A. What logic is: namely correct reasoning, or the study of correct reasoning.

  B. What logic is not: stoicism, absence of religious belief, science.

  C. God, by His nature, always thinks correctly, and therefore logically.

  D. Therefore, to study logic is to study the way God thinks.

Short Answer

1. What is the definition of logic?

2. What does logic have to do with God?

3. Is atheism a religious belief? Why or why not?

4. What is a question that can be answered logically, but not scientifically?

5. Can God say something false? Why or why not?

6. Can God learn anything new? Why or why not?

7. How is our thinking *like* God's thinking?

8. How is our thinking *unlike* God's thinking?

9. Using the words "discovers" and "determines," fill in the blanks to make the sentences true:

   Our mind _____ truth.

   God's mind _____ truth.

10. Can God be illogical? Why or why not?

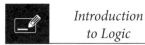
Chapter Review: This chapter covers epistemology: the study of how we know what is true. The Christian worldview has a distinct epistemology that separates it from other belief systems. Christian epistemology is revelational: meaning, we recognize that the only reason we are able to know anything at all is because God has given (revealed) some knowledge to us. This chapter expands on what we briefly covered in the previous chapter: that God's mind determines truth and is therefore the ultimate source for all knowledge. Our minds are merely the recipients of some knowledge. All truth exists in the mind of God, and no truth can be found outside of God's mind, because God's mind determines truth.

It is important to emphasize that this is one way in which our mind is not like God's. Explore both the similarities and differences between the mind of God and the mind of men. Similarities are due to the fact that we are made in God's image. Differences are due to the Creator/creature distinction.

This chapter also covers a possible objection to the claim that all knowledge comes from God. Namely, how then can atheists know anything? The answer is common grace. God has given some knowledge even to people who hate Him and verbally deny His existence. Even atheists really do know God in their heart-of-hearts, but suppress that truth in unrighteousness (Romans 1:18).

We also cover the fact that there are multiple ways to acquire knowledge, but they all ultimately depend on revelation from God. We can indeed learn from sensory experience, and from rational reflection. But our senses and our mind are both gifts from God and we could know nothing apart from Him.

Short Answer

1. Where does knowledge ultimately come from, and how do you know?

2. What is "revelation"?

3. What is "special revelation"?

4. What does "objective" mean?

5. What does "propositional" mean?

6. What are some ways in which human beings acquire knowledge?

7. How is our mind *like* God's?

8. How is our mind *unlike* God's?

9. If all knowledge is from God, then how are unbelievers able to know anything at all?

10. When non-Christians reason correctly, does this show that they do not need God to reason? Why/why not?

Chapter Review: This chapter is motivational in nature. There are two topics of focus. First, this chapter emphasizes and expands upon the Christian basis for logic as touched upon in chapters 1 and 2. Second, and as a consequence of this, students should want to learn logic, for they are literally learning how God thinks! The goal of this chapter is to motivate students to want to study logic. The chapter explores several reasons why we should delve into logic.

(A) The practical benefits of knowing logic, versus the consequences of failing to know logic. People want to think that their beliefs are correct. If you want your beliefs to actually be correct, you had better study logic. The flipside is that failing to understand logic will make you much more likely to be fooled. People really hate to be the fool, so emphasize this point strongly. The people who don't know logic are those that lose thousands of dollars to con artists. Knowing logic will make you a better thinker in whatever you study, from science and math to the Bible, because it applies to everyone no matter what they want to do career-wise.

(B) Logic is the study of the way God thinks. So, by studying logic, you are actually studying theology! This is a great point to emphasize for students who fancy themselves theologians, but are not terribly excited about logic. Students planning on going into ministry better learn something about the mind of the God they serve. Students of science better learn something about God's mind since it is God's mind that controls every atom in the universe. Knowing how their Creator thinks will give them an edge over secular students. Emphasize how awesome it is that we are learning about God's mind! It would be wonderful to learn how Leonardo da Vinci's mind worked, or Albert Einstein's. How much more awesome to learn about the mind of God!

(C) We have a moral obligation to be logical. It is not only impractical to fail to be logical; it is actually sinful. Conversely, right thinking is pleasing to God and results in His blessings. This will be a novel concept to most students. They could have guessed that logical thinking is advantageous, but few students realize that it is a biblical command to think in a way that is consistent with God's nature — which is what logic really is. Most of the chapter focuses on this last point since it is the least intuitive.

Short Answer

1. How do we know that it is possible for human beings to think in a way that is consistent with God's thinking?

2. Correct reasoning is not optional for a Christian but is in fact required. Why?

3. What are some practical advantages in learning to think logically?

4. According to Isaiah 55:7–8, what is the wicked man's basic problem?

5. According to Isaiah 55:7–8, what is the solution to the wicked man's problem?

6. What is an example of a time and place in which we should make an argument for the Christian faith?

7. What is an example of a time and place in which we should *not* make an argument for the Christian faith?

8. Give an example of a false statement that would lead to disaster if someone believed it.

9. Since God's thoughts are so superior to ours (as the heavens are higher than the earth — Isaiah 55:9), is it possible to ever think like God? If so, in what way(s)? If not, why not?

10. In what way(s) can logic be considered an aspect of theology?

Chapter Review: This chapter introduces the "argument" and the terminology of arguments. After reading this chapter, students should understand what an argument is, how it is used, and terms such as "proposition," "premise," and "conclusion." In logic, an argument is a good thing, not a bad thing; it's not a yelling match or an attempt to incite emotions, but a dispassionate analysis leading to a conclusion.

Students should learn to identify propositions, and to distinguish them from other kinds of sentences. A proposition is the meaning of claim, and that exact wording does not matter. This chapter introduces premises and conclusions, but these will be expanded upon in the next chapter.

Short Answer

1. What is logic?

2. What is an argument?

3. What are the two key characteristics of a good argument?

For each of the following, is the sentence a proposition?

4. You are crazy.

5. The night sky is beautiful.

6. Are you okay?

7. Please open the door.

8. The number of stars in the galaxy is an even number.

9. Most dogs are purple.

10. When exiting the theater, use the door on the right.

11. Is the square root of 4 equal to 2?

12. Blue is my favorite color.

13. Logic is fun!

For the following examples, answer these two questions: (A) Is this an argument? (B) If so, is it a reasonable argument or a bad argument?

14. All mammals have lungs, and all dogs are mammals, therefore all dogs have lungs.

15. The Bible is the Word of God.

16. Most scientists believe in Darwinian evolution, so you should too.

17. Since water is wet, and since watermelons have water on the inside, they must be wet on the inside.

18. Since it is free, why have you not yet bought the book?

Chapter Review: This chapter introduces students to the distinction between inductive and deductive arguments. Tip-off words and phrases like "probably, most likely, generally" are indicative of an inductive argument. But ultimately, one must ascertain whether the person making the argument is trying to make a probabilistic claim, or an absolute claim.

This chapter also introduces the term "fallacy," which will be greatly expanded upon in upcoming chapters. However, since chapter 4 contained a great deal of information to absorb, this chapter reviews some of that information, and expands on how to identify the premises and conclusions of an argument.

Short Answer

For the following, is the argument deductive or inductive?

1. Generally, men are faster runners than women. Therefore, the fastest human is probably male.

2. All plants contain chlorophyll. Flowers are plants. Therefore, flowers contain chlorophyll.

3. If it is snowing, then it must be cold outside. It is snowing. Therefore, it must be cold outside.

4. Dr. Lisle has not answered his phone all day. So, he is most likely out of the office.

5. Dogs do not have tails, and Spot is a dog, therefore Spot does not have a tail.

6. Smoking can lead to lung cancer. Doug has lung cancer. So he is probably a smoker.

For the following arguments, identify the premise(s) and the conclusion.

7. You should vote for Republicans because they better represent Christian values.

8. You really should go to church since the Bible tells you to in Hebrews 10:25.

9. We really shouldn't murder because it violates God's law.

10. My new dog is a golden retriever, so he will probably have a pleasant demeanor since most golden retrievers do.

11. All organisms are based on DNA, therefore they have descended from a common ancestor.

12. We know that smoking causes cancer. All the medical doctors say so.

13. There can be no doubt that all vertebrate animals share a common ancestor. After all, they all have certain anatomical similarities.

14. Stars must be very far away. They look so tiny.

Chapter Review: We have previously seen that the Bible indicates that God is the basis for logical reasoning. In this chapter, we expand on this by showing philosophically why God is the necessary prerequisite for having *laws* of logic. We examine the properties of laws of logic: they are universal, invariant, abstract entities. Only the mind of God as revealed in Scripture can make sense of these properties and also make sense of our ability to know that laws of logic have these properties. Namely, the sovereign, omnipresent, timeless nature of God's mind is why laws of logic exist and have the properties they have. That humans have been made in God's image is why we are able to think God's laws of logic like Him. And we know God's attributes because He has revealed them to us in Scripture.

Rather than leaving the laws of logic as example-less unknown conceptions, students are introduced to three of them. These are usually considered the three most fundamental laws of logic, often called the three laws of thought. Not only do laws of logic in general stem from the mind of God, but we can see how each of these three laws of thought specifically is rooted in the nature of God and are used throughout Scripture. We briefly cover the fact that non-biblical worldviews cannot make sense of the existence and properties of laws of logic, but we will leave the details until the next chapter.

Short Answer

For each of the following, write the negation of the stated proposition. Yes, this is as easy as it seems. You simply need to write "It is not the case that" in front of each of the following. The purpose is to drill home the nature of the negation.

1. All dogs are black.

2. Water is wet.

3. Blue is my favorite color.

For the following, which one of the three laws of thought is illustrated in the listed verse?

4. John 19:22

5. Matthew 12:30

6. 2 Corinthians 1:18

7. Mark 12:15

8. Romans 9:15

Which one of the three laws of thought is violated in the following examples?

9. "You actually can have your cake and eat it too."

10. "To be or not to be? I say neither!"

11. "My car is in the garage right now, and it is not in the garage right now."

12. "I am not really me."

Chapter Review: In this chapter we see that the existence and properties of laws of logic are evidence that the Christian worldview is correct. No alternative to Christianity can justify the existence and properties of laws of logic, because they are rooted in the nature of God as revealed in Scripture. This chapter is very valuable in apologetics because unbelievers like to think that they are very logical. But the concept of logic is rooted in God's character. Hence, the unbeliever must stand on Christian ground while simultaneously arguing against the Christian worldview. His position is self-defeating.

Short Answer

The first two questions may require the student to recall facts introduced in the previous chapter. You may want to remind the students that our study of logic is progressive, building on what came before. Therefore, students should occasionally reflect on earlier material so they do not forget it.

1. What characteristic of the biblical God makes sense of the fact that laws of logic are universal?

2. What characteristic of the biblical God makes sense of the fact that laws of logic are invariant?

3. What are some reasons why the laws of logic cannot merely be a reflection of the physical universe?

4. Why can the Muslim god Allah, as described in the Quran, not be the basis for laws of logic?

5. If the Greek gods were real, could they be the basis for the laws of logic? Why or why not?

6. Can the laws of logic be something that humans created? Why or why not?

7. Can a fictional god be the basis for the laws of logic? Why or why not?

8. Suppose some people invented a god called the "flying spaghetti monster." They claim that this god is responsible for the laws of logic. Would that god make sense of the laws of logic? Why or why not?

9. Suppose that these people claimed that the flying spaghetti monster was identical to the biblical God in every way, and therefore can make sense of laws of logic without appealing to the biblical God. Is their reasoning correct? Why or why not?

10. Someone says, "I have good reasons to believe that laws of logic are universal and invariant without God. They have always applied everywhere. I have used them at all times." Is the reasoning correct? Why or why not?

Chapter Review: Our goal in this chapter is really quite simple: help students properly understand the difference between *intuitive* and *logical*. I will grant that the Bible is often counterintuitive. But it is never illogical. People misuse these terms frequently. They might say that something is "illogical" when they really mean "counterintuitive." To be logical, something need only be in accordance with laws of logic. To be intuitive, something must make sense to us, and be according to our expectations. But often, our expectations are wrong. So, we dare not judge matters of truth by mere intuition. The problem is: most people judge something to be true or false based on intuition, rather than logical reasoning. This is an enormous problem in our post-modern culture.

The Bible is never illogical in what it affirms. We do allow that the Bible *correctly records* false claims or illogical arguments *by others*. Therefore, a second goal in this chapter is to help students to see that the Bible does not *affirm* everything it *records*. The Bible only affirms that people said what it records they said, but it does not necessarily affirm that what they said is true.

Short Answer

1. What is the difference between something being *logical* and being *intuitive*?

2. Besides Psalm 14:1, what is something that the Bible *records* but does not *affirm*? Provide the reference.

3. Name a biblical truth that most people find counter-intuitive.

4. The Trinity is the concept that God is one in His essential nature, and three in persons (Father, Son, Holy Spirit). Is the Trinity a contradiction? Why or why not?

5. When people make a logical argument with the conclusion "We should not make logical arguments," what law of logic are they violating?

6. Why is it impossible for the Bible to affirm two contradictory propositions?

Chapter Review: The takeaway of this chapter is that faith and reason are not contrary to each other as many people falsely assume, but in fact work together. Biblical faith is not an emotional leap in the dark, but is in fact the exact opposite. Biblical faith is reasonable / logical / rational. It is irrational to lack faith in the Bible because the biblical worldview is the necessary precondition for all the things necessary for human beings to reason, such as the basic reliability of our senses. The goal here is to counter the horrible misconceptions of biblical faith often espoused by critics of Christianity, i.e., that biblical faith is blind.

We also deal with biblical verses that are often misused to reinforce unbiblical conceptions of faith. For example, trusting in God with all your heart does not refer to an emotional feeling or irrational belief. Biblically, the heart represents the core of our being, and is more often associated with the mind — the seat of our consciousness — than with emotions. Likewise, those verses in Scripture that seem to promote the foolishness of Christianity are in reality promoting wisdom. The wisdom of God seems foolish to the secular world because the secular world is in fact foolish.

Short Answer

1. What is the biblical definition of faith?

2. Is it logical to have faith in God? Why or why not?

3. Is it logical to rely on emotions as a basis for truth? Why or why not?

4. Besides the physical organ, what does "heart" generally mean when used in Scripture?

5. Proverbs 4:5, 7 tells us to get *wisdom*, yet 1 Corinthians 1:21 tells us that God uses the *foolishness* of preaching to save people. Do these verses contradict? Why or why not?

6. If genuine wisdom always and only comes from God (Colossians 2:3; James 3:13–18), then are unbelievers able to have any wisdom? If so, how?

7. What are the requirements to being rational?

8. What is a biblical reason to believe that our sensory organs are basically reliable?

9. What is a biblical reason to believe that the universe has order, consistency, and repeating cycles?

Chapter Review: As we progress toward the section on fallacies, students are introduced to the two fundamental errors in reasoning that are behind all others: arbitrariness and inconsistency. One could argue that the entire point of education is to slay these two enemies of reasoning. Students should learn to have good, self-consistent reasons for their beliefs, and to relinquish beliefs that fail to have good, self-consistent reasons.

Often, knowing the name of a specific fallacy is unnecessary to spot a bad argument; if the argument is obviously arbitrary or inconsistent with itself, no further refutation is required. The goal in this chapter is to train the student to always ask these two questions: Do I have a good reason to believe this claim? Is the reasoning self-consistent? A "no" response to either of these provides a sufficient reason to reject a claim as dubious.

In a sense, these two aspects of reasoning are obvious and require little explanation. However, if anyone doubts that good reasoning should not be arbitrary, simply point out that the reverse leads to absurdity. Namely, if we don't need a reason to believe something, then we can believe literally anything no matter how obviously false. Likewise, if anyone doubts that reasoning should be self-consistent, point out that the alternative is self-refuting: if you don't need to be self-consistent then you do need to be self-consistent. The statement could only be refuted if self-consistency is required.

Short Answer

1. What are the two primary intellectual sins of all fallacious reasoning?

2. What does it mean to be arbitrary?

3. Are all forms of arbitrariness sinful? If not, provide an example. If so, why?

4. Give an example of sinful arbitrary reasoning.

5. What are some types of inconsistency?

6. Why is inconsistency to be avoided in rational reasoning?

7. How can refuting arbitrariness with arbitrariness be useful in a debate?

8. How can refuting inconsistency with inconsistency be useful in a debate?

9. Do we have a moral obligation to be consistent in our thinking? Why or why not?

10. Aside from the ones given in the chapter, give an example of behavioral inconsistency.

Chapter Review: We here introduce five types of definitions. Four of these are legitimate and useful in the construction of a logical argument. Emphasize that the dictionary is a very useful tool in debates, and indeed can settle debates when the topic concerns the way in which a word is used. Unlike matters of science and history, matters of definition are conventional — they are determined by the majority. A word means what the majority of people intend it to mean and will (eventually) be recorded in a dictionary or textbook.

Lexical, stipulative, precising, and technical definitions are often necessary to avoid miscommunication and errors in reasoning such as equivocation (discussed in a later chapter). Since this text focuses on logic, we presume that the students will mainly use existing definitions.

The fifth type of definition — the persuasive or rhetorical definition — is fallacious and is not ethical to use. However, students should be aware of this fallacy so that (1) they themselves do not commit it, and (2) they can spot the error when others commit it. The persuasive definition may indeed persuade. It often works. But its use is not only illogical, but also immoral, as it proposes a definition which is false.

Short Answer

Identify which type of definition is used in each of the following examples:

1. In a research paper: "By 'scientist' I mean anyone with a Ph.D. in a field of science who does research for a living."

2. Any definition found in a standard dictionary and not associated with any particular theory.

3. In a newspaper editorial: "Republican: any old white male afraid of change."

4. In a physics textbook: "Schwarzschild radius: the distance surrounding the singularity of a black hole at which no material can escape the gravitational pull of the singularity."

5. In a technical paper: "In honor of Dr. Buckminsterfuller, we have decided to designate this new form of carbon as Buckminsterfullerine."

6. "By 'evolution' I refer to the Darwinian idea of descent from a common ancestor."

Chapter Review: Although this course does not focus on formal logic, a brief introduction to syllogisms is necessary because so much of logic — even when used informally — is syllogistic in nature. Essentially, every syllogism attempts to connect two terms (the subject term and predicate term) to each other by linking them both to a middle term in some way. In terms of everyday conversations, people seldom use an explicitly stated syllogism. But people *often* use a syllogism with an unstated proposition — an enthymeme. The enthymeme will be the topic of the next chapter. The source of many an error in reasoning is found in the unstated proposition of an enthymeme. Therefore, it is necessary for students to understand the basics of categorical syllogisms, which is the goal of this chapter.

There are six rules that determine a correct syllogism, and therefore six fallacies associated with syllogisms — one for each broken rule. We will not cover these here because it goes beyond the scope of informal logic. However, students should be able to figure out whether a syllogism is valid or not by careful reflection.

Short Answer

1. Is it possible to have an argument that is invalid but sound? If so, give an example.

2. Is it possible to have an argument that is valid but unsound? If so, give an example.

For the following syllogisms, identify the subject term, the predicate term, and the middle term. Then put the following arguments in their abbreviated form (use a capital letter to represent each term).

3. All basketball players are very tall.

   All Celtics are basketball players.

   Therefore, all Celtics are very tall.

4. All Dallas Cowboys are football players.

   Some Texans are Dallas Cowboys.

   Therefore, some Texans are football players.

5. No fish have lungs.

   Some aquatic creatures are fish.

   Therefore, some aquatic creatures do not have lungs.

For each of the below arguments, indicate whether the argument is valid or invalid. Also indicate whether the argument is sound or unsound.

6. All humans are classified as mammals.

   All monkeys are classified as mammals.

   Therefore, some monkeys are classified as humans.

7. All men are mortal.

   Socrates is a man.

   Therefore, Socrates is mortal.

8. No creationists are scientists.

   Dr. Lisle is a creationist.

   Therefore, Dr. Lisle is not a scientist.

9. Some mammals have wings.

   All bats are mammals.

   Therefore, all bats have wings.

10. The Creator of the universe is God.

    Jesus is the Creator of the universe.

    Therefore, Jesus is God.

Chapter Review: The topic of enthymemes is not always covered in texts on informal logic. And yet it is one of the most common ways to conceal an error in reasoning. An enthymeme is an argument with an unstated premise or an unstated conclusion. They are extremely common in everyday arguments because people seldom state an argument in full. We use linguistic shortcuts. And there is nothing necessarily wrong with doing so. There is nothing inherently wrong with using an enthymeme. They are very practical.

However, enthymemes can be misused. And that is the main point of this chapter. Often when an enthymeme has a false proposition, it is the *unstated* proposition. This makes the error in reasoning harder to spot because it was never actually stated — merely implied. The goals for this chapter are for the student to (1) recognize an enthymeme, (2) supply the missing premise that would be necessary to make the argument valid, and (3) to assess whether the missing premise is reasonable.

Short Answer

For each of the following enthymemes, supply the missing premise or conclusion to make the argument valid/cogent. (The argument does not need to be sound.)

1. All scientists believe in evolution.

   And Dr. Dawkins is a scientist.

2. No moths have these bulbs at tip of their antennae.

   Therefore, this insect is clearly not a moth.

3. Rhode Island has a misleading name.

   Therefore, it does not exist.

4. Of course Tim is a creationist.

   He is a Christian after all.

5. In my opinion, God is very mean.

   Therefore, He does not exist.

6. It is sunny today.

   And it is usually clear on nights that follow sunny days.

7. Natural selection does not literally select anything.

   Therefore, it is not really real.

8. Of course you should tithe.
   The Bible says you should.

9. Whatever does not kill you will only make you stronger.
   And this certainly will not kill you.

10. All scientists with a Ph.D. must write a dissertation.
    So, obviously Kenny has written one.

Chapter Review: We here begin with an introduction to a major topic in informal logic: fallacies. Students should know something about errors in reasoning so that they will not commit these errors themselves and so that they will be able to spot the errors in arguments made by other people. Although this curriculum covers the main informal fallacies, particularly in the context of apologetics, students should know that informal fallacies are only part of the study of incorrect reasoning. Advanced students will want to go on and study formal logic and its associated fallacies.

This chapter introduces the students to the three major categories of informal fallacies: ambiguity, presumption, and relevance. The goal is for students to have a basic grasp of why these are errors, and be able to classify fallacies as belonging to one of these categories. Sometimes when a bad argument is presented, students new to logic will struggle to identify the fallacy. It will help narrow down the field if the student can at least identify the category. Does the error have to do with confusing wording? Ambiguity. Does the error involve making an assumption that is questionable? Presumption. Does the error involve something that is off-topic? Relevance. After the category is identified, it will be easier to narrow down the error to the specific fallacy.

Short Answer

Classify each of the following logical fallacies according to its category (ambiguity, presumption, or relevance):

1. An argument assumes something that is very questionable.

2. An argument makes a point that is true, but it is not the point the arguer is trying to make.

3. An argument uses a word in two different and inconsistent ways without clarification.

4. "Clearly, John is a registered Republican. Yesterday, he made several negative remarks about Hillary Clinton."

5. "Darwin believed in evolution. And we know that evolution is true because evolution means 'change' and things change every day."

6. "I wouldn't believe anything Joe says about government. He doesn't even pay taxes."

7. "Well of course Dr. Smith believes in evolution. He is a scientist after all."

8. "Practice makes perfect. And doctors practice medicine. Therefore, doctors are perfect."

Chapter Review: Equivocation can often be avoided by defining the key relevant terms at the outset of the debate or conversation and asking the other person to do the same. Ask, "What do you mean by ____?" Far and away the most common example of the equivocation fallacy in evolutionary arguments is the conflation of particles-to-people evolution with variation within a kind (which can be called "evolution"). This single fallacy occurs so often, that even if it were the only example of equivocation, it justifies this entire chapter.

Perhaps the second most common equivocation fallacy in origins debates concerns the meaning of the word "science." Does it mean the scientific method, the body of knowledge obtained by that method, a particular model, historical science, or origins science? Or is the term "science" being used fallaciously to refer to secular beliefs like evolution and deep time? Clarification is needed if proper communication is to be accomplished.

We do mention the fallacy of amphiboly in this chapter, but only for the sake of completeness. Namely, most textbooks on logic will include exactly the six fallacies of ambiguity listed in this text. However, in my experience, amphibolies are very rare in debates on worldview or origins. Usually, they occur in the context of an advertisement or article that has not been proofread carefully. They are usually funny, and rather obvious. Therefore, we will not ask students to focus on this topic, and do not include (intentional) amphibolies in the questions.

Short Answer

For each of the examples below, answer these two questions: (A) Is this an example of equivocation? (B) If so, which word is equivocated?

1. Science is a very powerful tool, so why deny the science of evolution?

2. Dr. Mitchell is a medical doctor. And doctors know a lot about medicine. So, it stands to reason that Dr. Mitchell knows a lot about medicine.

3. Charles Darwin believed in evolution. He understood that all life was descended from a common ancestor.

4. Creationists are badly mistaken. Evolution is a scientific fact. The evolution of bacteria becoming resistant is well-documented.

5. We don't deny the Bible, but it's your interpretation we believe to be wrong. We must always be sure that our interpretation of the Bible matches our interpretation of nature.

6. Science is what allows us to put men on the moon. And science is how we know what happened millions of years ago. You don't deny the first, so why deny the second?

7. Science is the way we learn about nature. That's why the science of astronomy is how we know so much about the universe.

8. Species are constantly evolving — adapting to their environment. The evolution of the SARS virus, the changes in allele frequency of many organisms, and the various breeds of dogs all demonstrate the truth of evolution. How can creationists honestly deny evolution?

9. Christians are Christ-followers. And Joseph claims to be a Christian. Therefore, he is really claiming to be a Christ-follower.

10. The Bible claims that God is omnipotent — that He can do anything He wants to do. Yet, the Bible also says that God cannot lie. Therefore, He is not really omnipotent.

Chapter Review: "Science says" and "evidence leads" are perhaps two of the most common uses of reification in debates over origins. The arguer may attempt to use this non-literal figure of speech to obscure an important fact in a debate — the fact that science is a tool and not a person, or that evidence requires interpretation. Many people have been fooled into believing something false by a bad argument containing a reification fallacy.

However, reification is tricky because (unlike equivocation) it is not always a fallacy. Reification in poetry is not only acceptable, but quite beautiful. Therefore, our two goals in this chapter are for students to (1) recognize reification, and (2) assess whether that reification is acceptable or fallacious. The main way to determine the former is to look for personification of inanimate objects or abstractions. The main way to determine the latter is to see if the reification occurs as part of a logical argument. An argument should be as clear as possible, and therefore should use language in a primarily literal way.

The fallacy of reification is also called "the fallacy of hypostatization" or "the fallacy of misplaced concreteness."

Short Answer

For each of the following, answer these three questions: "Is this an example of reification?" "Is it a fallacious use of reification?" and "Why or why not?" In each example, the key sentence is in italics.

1. "How is it that these microorganisms are able to thrive in boiling hot water? *Nature has found a way.*"

2. "Then what happened? Well, after fish evolved, *life invaded the dry land.*"

3. "You might wonder how chance processes could result in such remarkable features in organisms — features that may seem like they are designed. But remember, *natural selection guided the development of these organisms.*"

4. "You are appealing to God, which is a mistake. *Science says that we must limit explanations to the natural world.*"

5. The title of Duane Gish's book: "*Evolution: The Fossils Say No!*"

6. "We thought it would be sunny today, so we planned to have a picnic. *But nature had other plans.*"

7. "*Evolution tells us much about the way the world works.* Therefore, creationists should not reject it."

8. "You claim that science confirms the existence of God. *But you are mistaken because science is atheistic in its approach.*"

9. "Creationists say that life was supernaturally created. *But scientists know that life came about by natural processes.*"

10. "You should not interpret the data according to your biases. Rather, *follow the evidence where it leads.*"

Chapter Review: This chapter is brief because the fallacy of accent is easy to understand and does not occur commonly in worldview debates. But it does happen rarely and is included for completeness. A proposition is the meaning behind the words. Two different propositions can have exactly the same words, but they differ due to which words are emphasized. The chapter gives several illustrations of this. The goal is simply for students to recognize the fallacy of accent as it occurs in a debate.

The questions for this chapter will also challenge students to recall what they have learned in the previous chapters as they distinguish between the fallacy of accent, equivocation, and reification.

Short Answer

For each of the following, answer (A) Is this the fallacy of equivocation, reification, accent, or not a fallacy? And (B) Why?

1. "Feathers are very light. And light is the fastest substance. Therefore, feathers are the fastest substance."

2. Stacy normally gets groceries on Monday, but this week she gets groceries on Tuesday. On Wednesday she says to her friend Tammy, "I didn't get groceries on Monday this week." Tammy responds, "Really, who did?"

3. "Man is the only creature with a soul. And a woman is not a man. Therefore, a woman does not have a soul."

4. "You cannot travel faster than light. Nature will resist your every effort."

5. Brent has to cancel his date with Emily at the last minute due to a family emergency, so Emily stays home and watches television. Later, Courtney asks Emily, "How was your date with Brent?" Emily says, "I didn't go on a date with Brent." Courtney responds, "Oh, whom did you go with?"

6. "You really should file your income taxes. Fairness demands it."

7. Terry says, "It is impolite to talk bad about people behind their back."
   Pat says, "You really think it is wise to talk bad about people to their face?"

8. Paul says, "I've thought of asking Amy to marry me, but I'm not sure I really love her."
   Troy says, "Well, who do you love? Perhaps you should ask her instead."

9. "Rambunctious children are a real headache. Two aspirin will make a headache go away. Therefore, two aspirin will make rambunctious children go away."

10. "Religion is evil. It deceives people into thinking that there is an afterlife. It kills people through war. That's why I hate religion."

Chapter Review: It is vital to identify the conclusion of an argument. The conclusion can be stated first, or last, or even in the middle. The key is to identify what the writer/speaking is intending to establish (conclusion) as opposed to what he or she takes for granted (premises). This will distinguish between composition and division. Composition says something about the whole/group in the conclusion. Division says something about the parts/individuals in the conclusion.

Our goal here is for the students to identify whether something is a composition or division, and then to identify whether the composition or division is legitimate or fallacious. We ask, "Does the property in question transfer between the whole and parts, or does it not?" The examples should be helpful.

We also cover the important distinction between the distributive and the collective use of terms like "all." Does "all" mean "all the items taken together as a whole," or does it mean "each and every item considered one at a time"? Either use is legitimate. Context alone will distinguish between these uses. The fallacies of division and composition stem from a misunderstanding about whether a person is considering a distributive "all" or a collective "all."

Short Answer

For each of the following answer (A) Is this a fallacy of division, the fallacy of composition, or not a fallacy, and (B) why?

1. "Airplanes can't really fly. Think about it. They are made of millions of pieces — not one of which flies."

2. Every part of the universe has a cause. Therefore, the universe has a cause.

3. "People say the way to reduce our fossil fuel consumption is for more people to take the bus to work instead of driving their car. But that's absurd. Buses use a lot more gasoline than cars."

4. "Human beings have an immortal soul. And a finger is part of a human being. Therefore, a finger has an immortal soul, or at least part of a soul."

5. "I love hot salsa. But I also like chocolate. So, I would probably love chocolate dipped in salsa."

6. "No atoms are alive. And people are made of atoms. Therefore, people are not alive."

7. Tim: "Some people have survived all types of cancer." Renae: "Not true. I doubt anyone has even had every type of cancer, let alone survived them all."

8. A coach says to his track team, "If a person runs faster, he can win a race. So, if all of you run faster, you can all win the race."

9. "Every part of the universe obeys laws of nature. Earth is part of the universe. Therefore, earth obeys laws of nature."

10. "The brain is the seat of human consciousness and is comprised of millions of synapses. Therefore, each synapse must be a little bit conscious."

| Introduction to Logic | Hasty Generalization and Sweeping Generalization | Days 88-89 | Chapter 19 Worksheet 19 | Name |

Chapter Review: This begins the section on fallacies of presumption. The common feature of fallacies in this category is that they presume something that is questionable. Sometimes these fallacies can be "fixed" by supplying additional information to bolster the presumed claim.

Reasoning often involves the use of generalizations — patterns that apply most of the time, and in some cases, all of the time. Sometimes people reason from a generalization to conclude something about a specific instance. And sometimes they do the reverse — they reason from several specific instances to conclude something about a generalization. Both of these are legitimate uses of reason, providing we keep in mind an important caveat: generalizations often have exceptions.

The hasty generalization uses instances to draw a conclusion about a generalization, but does so with insufficient instances. Hence, there is no way to know whether the instances are typical, or exceptions. Conversely, the sweeping generalization starts with the generalization, and applies it to a specific instance that happens to be an exception. The goal in this chapter is have the students recognize the hasty and sweeping generalization fallacies and to distinguish the difference between the two.

The key is to recognize that the sweeping generalization starts with the generalization as a premise and reasons to a specific instance in the conclusion, whereas the hasty generalization starts with specific instances and falsely concludes a generalization.

Short Answer

For each of the following answer (A) Is this a hasty generalization, a sweeping generalization, or not a fallacy? and (B) Why?

1. "The Bible states that Noah was to bring two of every animal on board the ark (Genesis 6:19–20). But later it contradicts this by saying that seven of some animals were brought on board (Genesis 7:2)."

2. "Our local Christian school teaches creation, and their test scores are below average. So, clearly creationist thinking tends to be associated with low test scores."

3. "The Bible says that a soft, gentle answer turns away wrath (Proverbs 15:1). But John spoke gently to Henry yesterday, and Henry got angry anyway. So clearly the Bible is wrong."

4. "Kim and Julie are sisters, and they look very much alike. Apparently, sisters tend to look alike."

5. "People who are very closely related have very similar DNA. Clearly, similarities in DNA show that organisms are all related (this is why humans and chimpanzees have such similar DNA)."

6. Carl says, "You cannot legally yell 'fire' in a movie theater if there is no actual fire." Brenda responds, "Sure I can. I have the right to free speech. It's in the constitution!"

7. "That's the third time this week that a woman has lied to me! I guess you just can't trust women!"

8. "Big cities with little wind tend to have a lot of problems with smog. Los Angeles is an enormous city and doesn't have a lot of wind. So it most likely has problems with smog."

9. "All the planets and known asteroids in our solar system obey Kepler's three laws of planetary motion. Apparently, Kepler's laws are true and work at all times."

10. "We know that Jesus did not really walk on water, because water is liquid, and science shows that people cannot walk on a liquid surface."

Chapter Review: In this chapter, we explore cause-and-effect, and ask how can we establish that two events are causally connected. Causation is necessary succession — two events are causally connected if they happen in temporal order and if one event must follow the other given the circumstances. Succession is rather easy to see. But how do we establish that such succession is necessary? A complete answer goes beyond this text. Suffice it to say that this is one of the main purposes of science.

Even without a complete discussion on what is needed to reasonably conclude a cause-and-effect relationship, students should understand that mere correlation or succession is not enough. Just because two things happen at about the same time or go together does not necessarily mean that one has caused the other. More information is needed to establish causality. We cannot conclude that event A is the cause of event B, just because A happens before B — the *post hoc ergo propter hoc* fallacy. Nor can we conclude that just because two things go together that one is the cause of the other — the *cum hoc ergo propter hoc* fallacy. Students should be able to identify these fallacies.

We also delve into the topic of superstition, and the fact that it is rooted in the false cause fallacy. Students should come to realize that superstition is inherently irrational. It's not merely a fun tradition, but is contrary to logical thinking, and therefore foolish and displeasing to God.

Short Answer

For each of the following, answer (A) Is this a false cause fallacy? (B) If so, is it *post hoc ergo propter hoc, cum hoc ergo propter hoc,* **or neither? (C) Why?**

1. "As the sun vanished during the solar eclipse, the natives beat their drums continuously, hoping to cause the sun to return. It worked."

2. "Shortly after the school changed its policy and allowed teachers to carry concealed handguns, one of the students arrived, armed, and began shooting up the place. Clearly, this policy was a bad idea."

3. "Jim studied much harder this year for his SATs. And his score was much higher. Clearly, his studying paid off."

4. "Whenever I eat dairy products, I tend to get bloated and have stomach pains. I think I might be lactose intolerant."

5. "Over several decades, the environment got colder. And the animals now living there have thicker fur than the animals did when it was warmer. Clearly, these animals have self-adjusted to their environment."

6. "Humans and apes have very similar anatomy. This is because they have evolved from a common ancestor."

7. "Japan has the second highest percentage of atheists. And it has one of the lowest crime rates in the world. Clearly atheism is good for society."

8. "This wooden board is vibrating for some reason, but whenever I put a heavy book on it, the vibration stops. See? Whatever the cause, apparently placing a book on the board will make it stop vibrating."

9. "My cousin got this chain letter in the mail, but he didn't forward it on. Two weeks later, he had a fatal heart attack. Don't tell me chain letters don't do anything!"

10. "Whenever I get a headache, it lasts for days unless I take an aspirin. That aspirin really works to relieve my headache."

Chapter Review: The topics of begging the question and circular reasoning deserve two chapters due to the unusual nature of this method of argumentation. Two things are strange about circular reasoning: (1) it is valid, and (2) it is not always fallacious. However, almost all examples of begging the question and circular reasoning are fallacious, and it is the fallacious use of begging the question that we cover in this chapter. Only at very advanced levels of reasoning regarding a transcendental claim will legitimate uses of circular reasoning come into play, and only then if done properly.

There is a subtle difference between begging the question and circular reasoning. Circular reasoning technically involves two (or more) arguments where the conclusion of one is used as a premise in the other. Begging the question simply means that the conclusion of an argument or arguments is tacitly or explicitly assumed in a premise. We do not introduce that distinction to the students in this text, and indeed some people use the terms interchangeably.

One goal in this chapter is to educate students to identify fallacious examples of begging the question. Another equally important goal is to show students that all attempts to justify uniformity in nature (of the inductive principle) apart from the Christian worldview commit the fallacy of begging the question. This is a remarkable truth and serves as a proof of the Christian worldview. Namely, no competing worldview can justify our expectation that past experience is a good indicator of future successes, or that the future will be like the past in terms of the basic cycles of nature.

This is a difficult concept for students because we are accustomed (even "hard-wired") to believe in uniformity in nature and use it unconsciously. Hence, we have a tendency to unconsciously assume uniformity in nature even when trying to prove it — which of course begs the question! Students will have difficulty with this, so think through this issue carefully, and be prepared to explain it. The quote by Copi and Cohen in this chapter may be very helpful, as it is masterfully articulated.

Short Answer

For each of the following answer: (A) Does this argument beg the question? (B) Why or why not?

1. "Evolution must be true. After all, it is a well-established fact of science."

2. "We have confidence in the methods of science and induction because they have served us so well in the past."

3. "The moon shines by reflected sunlight. We know this because when the earth comes between the sun and moon (a lunar eclipse), the moon goes dark."

4. "I realize that evolution from single-celled organisms to people by mutations and natural selection may seem unlikely. But it is obviously true because we are here."

5. "We know that creation is true because it is part of recorded biblical history, and the history of the Bible has been confirmed by other historical sources and archaeology."

6. "How do we know that laws of physics are universal? Because everywhere on earth we've tested them, they work quite well. So it is reasonable to assume they are the same elsewhere."

7. "Creation cannot be true because it involves the supernatural."

8. "The Bible must be true because it says it is the Word of God, and God would not lie."

9. "The Quran must be true because it says it is the Word of God, and God would not lie."

10. "We don't actually need evidence for evolution, because it is a fact."

Chapter Review: This will likely be one of the most challenging chapters for students because it involves transcendental arguments: those arguments that deal with very basic truth claims. The goal is for students to be able to distinguish between virtuous and vicious circular arguments. Almost all circular arguments that will be encountered in ordinary contexts are vicious. But those arguments that attempt to either establish or refute foundational truth claims (such as laws of logic, induction, existence, etc.) will necessarily have to use those very claims as part of the argument. This is not an error. Rather, it is essential.

They key to distinguishing between a virtuous circular argument and a vicious one is arbitrariness. Vicious circular arguments arbitrarily assume the thing they are attempting to prove. Virtuous circular arguments establish that their own assumptions are justified by the impossibility of the contrary. Namely, any counterargument would have to assume the same thing the original argument did, thereby refuting itself. The classic example of this is included in the chapter: that any argument against the existence of laws of logic would have to use them. Immanuel Kant argued that it is reasonable to believe something if one would have to assume it in order to argue against it.

Short Answer

The following arguments all have a degree of circularity. For each, answer these questions: (A) Is the circle *virtuous* or *vicious/fallacious*? (B) Why or why not.

1. "Words must exist. Without them, we could not even say that words do not exist."

2. "Creation must be true because we are here."

3. "Laws of logic must be a legitimate way to reason; without them, we couldn't reason at all."

4. "We know laws of logic will work tomorrow because if they didn't, we wouldn't be able to reason tomorrow."

5. "We know that God is honest; He made our minds and our senses, so if God were dishonest, we could not trust our mind and senses and would therefore not know anything at all."

6. "We know that the big bang happened because the universe is here."

7. "We know our senses are basically reliable because evolution would tend to weed out organisms that have unreliable senses."

8. "Rock layers prove that the Bible is not true because they are deposited gradually over hundreds of millions of years."

9. "We know that laws of nature will work in the future as they did in the past, because in the past it was that way. Therefore, in the future it will be that way."

10. Someone says, "Air must exist because anyone attempting to argue against air would have to use air to voice his argument."

Chapter Review: The fallacy of the question-begging epithet is extremely common in debates over origins. For that matter, it is probably the most common fallacy among children in arguments on any topic. Children very quickly learn to use biased language to persuade or manipulate people. Politicians also use biased language to persuade. It is crucial to learn to spot biased language. That is the goal of this chapter. Students should learn to spot language that is subtly pushing them to believe something without making a rational argument.

Granted, some degree of bias is probably unavoidable. However, a rational argument must use logic, not mere rhetoric to draw a rational conclusion. Note that question-begging-epithets may be effective; they might indeed persuade people. But they are not rational. They do not help people draw a correct conclusion based on good reasons. Epithets subtly influence the mind to think in a particular way — a way that might have nothing to do with reality.

It is also noteworthy that biased or emotional language does have its place. It's not always wrong. Sometimes it is appropriate to stir a person's emotion by, for example, pointing out the atrocity of abortion. To think that someone would hire a hitman to assassinate a baby is abhorrent. And it is appropriate to say so. However, the point is that such loaded language is not a substitute for rational thought. When thinking through an issue, we should be as objective as possible so as to come away with a logical conclusion and not be swept away by our (frequently irrational) feelings. After we have reasoned through an issue as objectively as possible, and have drawn a reasonable conclusion, then it may be appropriate to stir others to action by rhetoric. The error that people commit is in substituting rhetoric for logic.

Television commercials often contain question-begging epithets. It might make a good (and fun) classroom exercise to examine some commercials.

Short Answer

For each of the following, answer these questions: (A) Is this a question-begging epithet fallacy? (B) Why or why not? (C) If so, is there a more objective way to argue the point and what would that be?

1. "Evolution vs. creationism."

2. "Creation vs. science."

3. "I will demonstrate that the facts of science are consistent with the model I have proposed."

4. "Creation is so obviously wrong that I don't need to even argue my position!"

5. (vulgar language)

6. "The scientific position is evolution. Creation is just religious nonsense."

7. "God is arguably the most unpleasant character in all of fiction."

8. "We will show that creation is not consistent with the scientific data in the field of genetics."

9. "Why do I not believe in creation? Because I'm intelligent."

Long Answer

10. "I used to have blind faith just like you, but then I 'evolved.'"

Chapter Review: This error also uses biased language to smuggle in an unproved claim. Students may confuse this with the question-begging epithet. The difference is easy to spot: the epithet ends in a period (or exclamation point), whereas the complex question ends in a question mark. It's just that simple. (The confusion may stem from the fact that the previous two fallacies also have the word "question" in them.)

As with the previous chapter, the goal is for students to learn to spot instances where they are being pressed to accept a claim by biased language rather than logical reasons.

Short Answer

All of the following are examples of the complex question. For each, divide the question into two questions to eliminate the fallacy.

1. "If creation is true, then why does all the evidence point to evolution?"

2. "If the world is young, then why does it look so old?"

3. "Why are creationists against science?"

4. "Are you aware of the fact that evolution has been demonstrated in a laboratory?"

5. "How did life arise from random chemicals and diversify into all the species we see on earth today?"

6. "How is it that scientists are able to probe the distant past, and learn what life was like millions of years ago?"

7. "When are you going to stop believing nonsense and accept science?"

8. "Why are creationists so ignorant of the facts?"

9. "What is the mechanism by which birds evolved their wings?"

10. "Why is evolution so important to our understanding of biology?"

Chapter Review: This fallacy is also called the either-or fallacy and the false dilemma. It would be helpful for students to learn these other names for this fallacy because it will help them to remember what the fallacy is. Namely, when a claim is made "either A or B" we should always think to see if there is a possible third alternative. Sometimes there isn't, and therefore it's not a fallacy. But often — very, very often — a critic will present us with only two options, when the truth is an unstated third. Our goal in this chapter is to have students recognize that sometimes there are more possibilities than the few that are being presented.

The bifurcation fallacy is like being given a multiple-choice test, where the right answer is not listed. Students should learn to expect these from critics, and be able to point out the error by supplying the correct, third alternative.

Short Answer

For each of the following, answer: (A) Is this the fallacy of bifurcation? (B) If so, what is a possible third alternative?

1. "Either evolution is true, or everything we know about the world is wrong."

2. "Either you have reasons for what you believe, or you simply take it on faith."

3. "I could never be a creationist, because I'm rational."

4. "Either you believe in God, or you are an atheist."

5. "Do you believe the universe is governed by natural laws, or do you believe it is upheld by the hand of God?"

6. "The grass is wet. So it is either raining outside or someone left the sprinklers on."

7. "Either you are with me, or you are not."

8. "I listen to the Holy Spirit to tell me what to do, not the text of the Bible."

9. "Is God in control of everything that happens, or do we have freedom of choice?"

10. "Those who say they disbelieve Darwinian evolution are either misinformed or dishonest."

Chapter Review: This chapter is a great place to review the various types of definitions covered in chapter 11. All instances of the no true Scotsman fallacy occur when the arguer tacitly uses a rhetorical definition, not a legitimate definition. Explain to the students to watch for words like "real," "true," "legitimate," "genuine," and "actual." While these words have legitimate uses, they are a warning flag that we should look to see if this fallacy has been committed.

The goal here is for the students to recognize the no true Scotsman fallacy. When a person adds "real," "true," or some similar word to a noun to tacitly redefine it in a way that is not found in any dictionary, this fallacy is committed. The best way to refute a no true Scotsman fallacy is therefore with a dictionary.

For the first five questions for this chapter, we take a break from the usual "is this a fallacy?" approach to an exercise where students are encouraged to *create* a fallacy. This is not because such a fallacy is acceptable, but rather so the students can see how almost any argument can be constructed using this error. This should make the error much easier to spot when it occurs. The remaining five questions ask whether the fallacy occurs, which requires the students to investigate whether the correct definition of a word is in use.

Short Answer

For these questions, you get to be fallacious! How would a person use the no true Scotsman fallacy to fallaciously "refute" the following claims?

1. "Of course some dogs are black. Spot is a dog, and he is black."

2. "Many scientists believe the Bible. Look at the scientists in the Biblical Science Institute."

3. "Several technical journals publish creationist articles. Consider the *ARJ* or the *CRSQ*."

4. "Of course Christians can believe in evolution. Joe is a Christian and believes in evolution."

5. "Faith doesn't have to be 'blind.' My faith in the Bible is very rational."

For each of the following, answer: (A) Is this a true Scotsman fallacy, and (B) Why or why not?

6. "No real scientist would ignore the scientific method."

7. "No real Christian would embrace evolution."

8. "There is no real evidence that dogs have ever been anything but dogs."

9. "No true scholar would accept the Bible as a legitimate source of historical information."

10. "No true American would vote for a Democrat."

Chapter Review: This fallacy is particularly interesting because the Bible has quite a lot to say about the sin of using a double-standard. Hypocrisy is a type of special pleading — when a person's behavior does not match his words. When people expect others to behave in a way that they themselves are unwilling to do, this is special pleading. An evolutionist will often insist that we must only cite literature that agrees with evolution — with his beliefs. Yet, he will not allow the creationist to cite literature consistent with the creationist's beliefs. This is inconsistent. Inconsistency is one of the primary intellectual sins that defines irrationality.

Not all exceptions are special pleading. Some standards only apply in certain instances. And it is not a fallacy to point this out. The key is to discern whether the exception is justified or arbitrary. When a person arbitrarily exempts himself from a standard, this is special pleading.

Short Answer

For each of the following, is this an example of special pleading? Why or why not?

1. Craig says, "The Bible says you are not supposed to gamble."

   John responds, "It's okay because I plan to donate half my winnings to the church."

2. Jim says, "You are not supposed to work on Sunday. Yet you just gave a 45-minute public speech!"

   Bill responds, "But I'm the pastor."

3. A police officer pulls over a civilian for speeding and starts to give him a ticket.

   The civilian responds, "Could you let me off the hook? I'm really late for a church meeting."

4. A police officer pulls over a civilian for speeding and starts to give him a ticket.

   The civilian responds, "But my wife is having a heart attack and I'm trying to get her to the hospital."

5. "Evolution is so well-established that we don't need to support it with evidence at this point."

6. "You can't rely on the Bible for historical information! You must check ancient historical documents to find out what really happened."

7. "Yes, Christ's Resurrection may not be consistent with the laws of nature as we understand them. But it was a miraculous event."

8. Greg: "The same Bible teaches that God created in six days, and that Jesus rose from the dead. You believe the latter, why not the former?"

   Jeff: "That's different. The Resurrection of Christ was a miracle."

9. "You must not impose your morality on other people."

10. "You must use information from textbooks or peer-reviewed articles to support your case. Information from articles at the Biblical Science Institute does not count."

Chapter Review: Since both of these fallacies are relatively easy to spot, we include both in the same chapter. The first goal is for students to understand reasoning by analogy, and to compare and contrast the topic/item under discussion with the analogy representing it. In what ways are they similar? In what ways are they different? A good analogy will draw an inference from the ways in which the items are similar. A false analogy will draw an erroneous inference due to trivial, non-relevant, or apparent similarities. Students should be able to distinguish a good analogy from a false analogy.

Finally, we analyze the concept of the slippery slope. Some slippery slopes are legitimate. A particular action really is likely to cause another, then another, resulting in a particular outcome. But in other cases, other factors will be likely to prevent the stated outcome. The goal is for students to distinguish between a reasonable slippery slope and a fallacious one.

Short Answer

For each of the following, answer: (A) Is this a false analogy, a slippery slope fallacy, or neither? (B) and why?

1. "If we teach children that God created the universe in six days, then they will not be curious about how it really happened, and they will not pursue a career in science."

2. "Evolution is easy to understand. Just as cars today are not the same as cars 50 years ago, so organisms today are not the same as organisms 50 million years ago."

3. "If we teach children that they are merely evolved animals, then when they are older (barring any teaching to the contrary), they will be inclined to act like animals."

4. "Solar panels are a good alternative to fossil fuel. If more people would switch to solar panels, then it would reduce pollution, and save money in the long term."

5. "You believe in God just like little children believe in the tooth fairy."

6. "Just as we are able to read a clock and know the time, we can 'read' the radioactive elements in a rock and tell how old it is."

7. "All human beings begin life as a single cell which eventually develops into an adult. So it is very reasonable to think that all life evolved from a single-celled organism like a bacterium."

8. "Humor is like a frog. You can dissect it, but it will die in the process."

9. "No, you can't have another dog. If I were to get you another dog, then pretty soon, you'd want another, and then another. And we cannot handle a house full of dogs!"

10. To believe in creation is like believing that magical, invisible elves are responsible for making grass grow by pulling on it when you're not looking.

Chapter Review: In this review, we emphasize what all fallacies of presumption have in common. They assume something essential to the conclusion that has not been established. As such, each of these fallacies can be answered with a phrase something like, "But that assumes _____." The blank will be different for each fallacy, and we go through examples for each fallacy in this chapter. The questions ask students to distinguish between any of the fallacies within this section — fallacies of presumption.

Short Answer

For each of the following, identify the fallacy (if there is one) and explain why it is or is not fallacious.

1. "The evidence for evolution is simply overwhelming. Evidence from genetics, from paleontology, and from anatomy, all support the fact that all organisms share a common ancestor."

2. "Life is abundant on earth; almost every possible environment is filled with living organisms. So it is reasonable to conclude that life in space is also quite common."

3. "Science is all about what is observable and testable. That's why creation cannot be considered as science; you cannot observe the past. Clearly, evolution is the scientific position."

4. "If you are going to make an argument for creation, you have to use real, mainstream journals, not creationist ones."

5. "To deny that evolution takes place would be like denying the existence of gravity."

6. "People just don't come back to life. Go check out a cemetery. So it just isn't possible for Jesus to have been raised from the dead."

7. "We allowed the students to discuss alternatives to evolution this year and the science test scores were below normal. Do you see what allowing creationist ideas into the classroom does?"

8. "We don't know if birds evolved from the ground up or from the trees down."

9. "God may exist. But we must do science as if He does not. Otherwise, we would never know if we are studying the natural world, or a miracle. Science would come to a standstill."

10. "What is the probability that life could arise by chance? It must be 100 percent because we are here, after all."

Chapter Review: We now come to fallacies of relevance. These are fallacies in which the conclusion is not strongly relevant to the topic under discussion. As such, they do not rationally establish what the person is trying to accomplish. First in this section we have the *ad hominem* fallacy, or *ad hominem* attack. As included in the student text, the term is Latin and means "to the man." All of these fallacies have fancy Latin names, but we have been generous and used only the more common English name. However, this fallacy is always called by its Latin name.

Understanding the term *ad hominem* explains the fallacy — an argument directed against a person rather than the position the person holds. Negative political ads are often full of this fallacy, and you might want to show a few to the students to demonstrate this. The unethical fallacy often works; people are often persuaded not to accept an argument because there is something objectionable about the person making the argument. But this is irrational (and immoral). An argument stands or falls on its own merit. The person making the argument is utterly irrelevant.

The goal here is for students to learn to identify the *ad hominem* fallacy when it occurs, and to distinguish between the abusive *ad hominem*, and the circumstantial *ad hominem*. An important key to understanding the latter is this: just because a person is motivated to make an argument does not mean his argument is wrong. It may in fact be very good. But the argument itself must be investigated, not the person making it.

Another issue that we deal with in this chapter is to distinguish between a cause and a reason. The cause of a belief is not always the same thing as the reason for it. A cause is one of the chain of events in the universe that resulted in a person having a belief. A reason is the rational justification for the belief. All beliefs have a cause, but not all have reasons. Take superstitions for example. There is a cause for a person believing something silly. But there is no good reason for it. The circumstantial *ad hominem* fallacy often confuses causes with reasons.

Short Answer

For each of the following, answer these two questions: (A) is this an *ad hominem* fallacy? (B) If so, is it a circumstantial *ad hominem*, or an abusive *ad hominem*? If it is not a fallacy, why not?

1. "If you don't believe in evolution, then you're pretty much just a moron!"

2. "The witness claims to be the defendant's alibi. But we have shown that this witness is a notorious liar. So, his testimony should be considered unreliable."

3. "Creationists are really uneducated; you shouldn't bother listening to their arguments."

4. "The reason you believe in creation is because you were raised in a Christian home."

5. "You think we should allow the government to confiscate our guns? That's what Hitler believed! So, clearly you are wrong."

6. "Dr. Jones has drawn some incorrect conclusions because he used inaccurate records."

7. "The folks at the Biblical Science Institute argue for creation because it is how they make money."

8. "You simply believe in God as an intellectual crutch. You cannot stand the thought of being alone in the universe, so you invent an imaginary friend."

9. "You only disagree with me because you are a racist."

10. "Dr. Johnston has only published one paper in the technical literature; so his research is suspect."

Chapter Review: This chapter may challenge some students because not all appeals to authority are fallacious. Hence, I refer to the error as the *faulty* appeal to authority. It is perfectly appropriate to cite an expert in support of a particular theory or idea. But there are several ways in which this can be done fallaciously. We cover three such ways in this chapter.

The most difficult way to understand is perhaps the second: failure to consider the worldview of an expert. This will require students to think a bit about worldviews and how they affect our interpretation of data. This isn't easy, but it is an important aspect of apologetics. I cannot overstate the importance of being able to analyze worldviews, as this is at the very heart of defending the faith well. So take some time with this.

The goal is for students to be able to distinguish correct appeals to an expert, versus fallacious appeals, and to articulate why. We also cover the appeal to majority, which is always fallacious because majority belief does not determine truth.

Short Answer

For each of the claims below, answer: (A) Is this the fallacy of appeal to authority? (B) If so, in which of the three ways (mentioned in this chapter) does the argument fail?

1. "If creation is true, then why do the vast majority of scientists believe in evolution?"

2. "Of course evolution is true. Pretty much every biology textbook says so."

3. "Dr. So-and-so believes in evolution. So clearly it is true."

4. "The scientific consensus is that the world is billions of years old." (Implying: "Therefore we should believe this as well.")

5. "Of course all life evolved from a common ancestor. How could all those scientists be wrong?"

6. "You trust what the scientists say about gravity, electricity, chemistry, etc. Why do you doubt what they say about evolution?"

7. "Jim is one of the smartest people I know. And he believes in evolution." (Implying: "Therefore, we should too.")

8. "We know that the universe was created in six days because God says so in Genesis 1, and Exodus 20:11."

9. "Many Bible scholars believe that the days in Genesis are merely symbolic of longer periods of time, perhaps hundreds of millions of years each."

10. "We know salvation is only possible through Jesus because the Bible says so."

Chapter Review: A common debate tactic is to misrepresent your opponent's position to make it appear absurd and easy to refute. This is not only irrational, it is unethical. We have a moral obligation to present our opponent's view fairly. That doesn't mean we have to present it in a flattering way, only in an honest way. Some views are ridiculous — such as molecules to man evolution — and it is not a fallacy to say so. Nonetheless, we have a moral obligation to be honest about what our opponents claim. Even if a misrepresentation is unintentional, it is our obligation to study what our critics teach before we begin to refute their position. So our first goal is to ensure that students do not commit the strawman fallacy in arguments that we make. This is unacceptable for a Christian. Granted, misunderstandings will sometimes happen. But we should take reasonable effort to represent any opposing position as accurately as possible.

Our second goal is for students to recognize strawman arguments when other people make them. This can occur in an argument against Christianity, or it can occur in an argument against a third-party position. A strawman argument can of course occur in an argument against someone who holds a false position, and it may succeed in swaying people not to believe something that is false. However, the ends do not justify the means.

Spotting a strawman fallacy is really pretty straightforward, as long as you thoroughly understand the position. To recognize strawman arguments against the Christian position, we must therefore thoroughly understand the Christian position. To ensure that we do not commit a strawman fallacy in arguing against some non-biblical standard, we must study in order to carefully understand this other standard. Knowledge of the respective positions and precise use of language can reduce occurrences of this fallacy, and better enable us to spot it.

Since spotting a strawman fallacy is as easy (or difficult) as knowing the position, we have changed from the usual type of questions.

Short Answer

1. Give an example of a strawman fallacy that a critic of the Bible might say.

2. Is a strawman fallacy immoral? Why or why not?

3. A common strawman fallacy is: "Creationists don't believe in science." Why might this fallacy be so common?

4. How can we avoid making strawman fallacies in our own arguments?

5. What are some ways we can reduce the number of strawman fallacies that non-Christians tend to make in regard to Christianity?

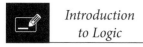
Chapter Review: The fallacies in this section are similar in that they appeal to something that is not relevant to the conclusion of an argument. Our goal is for students to be able to spot these fallacies, distinguish them from others (e.g., appeal to force versus appeal to emotion), and to refute them. Of special importance is the appeal to ignorance, a common fallacy that frustrates many people because they don't know how to refute it. But the appeal to ignorance can always be refuted with another appeal to ignorance. Galileo's example at the end of the chapter should help the students understand this approach.

Short Answer

For each of the following, (A) identify the fallacy; is it the appeal to fear/force, the appeal to emotion, the appeal to pity, the appeal to ignorance, or not a fallacy? (B) Explain why.

1. "The Oort cloud must exist. After all, no one has proved that it doesn't."

2. "If you want to continue to work at this company, you must believe the things we believe."

3. "I'm so worthless. No one believes me or agrees with me. Except you. You agree with me, don't you?"

4. "You should be a Republican. To be a Republican is to be an American. We represent freedom and democracy."

5. "You seriously believe the Bible? You really believe in a book written by uneducated goat herders who didn't even have indoor plumbing?"

6. "Darwinian evolution is very well-established. Even after nearly two hundred years, no one has been able to disprove it."

7. "But professor, you just have to give me a passing grade! If you don't, I won't graduate!"

8. "There are probably an infinite number of universes in the multi-verse. No one has provided any evidence to the contrary."

9. "You believe that we should surrender all our guns to the government? That's what Hitler believed."

10. "The law of gravity is very well-established. For centuries, it has allowed us to correctly predict the positions of planets in advance."

| *Introduction to Logic* | The Naturalistic, Moralistic, and the Appeal... | Days 153-154 | Chapter 34 Worksheet 34 | Name |

Chapter Review: These three fallacies conflate what is true from what is morally right or desirable. Not only do these fallacies occur frequently in debates, but they highlight an essential defect in all non-Christian worldviews: the inability to justify objective moral standards. The concepts of an objective "right" and "wrong" make no sense apart from the biblical God.

"Right" is that which God approves of, and "wrong" is that which God disapproves of. But when God is removed from the picture, "right" and "wrong" are reduced to mere subjective preferences and cannot therefore have any obligatory power on other people. God is the connection between what is right and what is true. God approves of that which is right, and decrees that which is true. Apart from God, there can be no connection between morality and reality.

The goal is for students to distinguish between what is true and what is right and to recognize that one does not imply the other. Students should be able to distinguish the naturalistic fallacy from the moralistic. Again, it will be helpful to identify the conclusion first. If the conclusion is making a moral claim based simply on what is true, then this is the naturalistic fallacy. Conversely, if the conclusion is making a claim about what is the case based on what would be morally right, it's the moralistic fallacy. If the conclusion makes a claim about reality merely based on what would be desirable or undesirable, it is the appeal to consequences. If students have difficulty distinguishing between these, help them first identify the conclusion of the argument, then look at which premises are used as support.

Short Answer

For each of the following, answer: (A) Is this the moralistic fallacy, the naturalistic fallacy, the appeal to consequences, or not a fallacy? (B) Why?

1. "I think everyone goes to heaven when they die regardless of whether they believe in Jesus. After all, the alternative is too horrible to even contemplate."

2. "Look, pirating movies from the Internet can't be wrong. Everyone does it."

3. "Smoking can lead to heart disease, and lung cancer. All the doctors say so."

4. "You really shouldn't lie. It is contrary to the Bible."

5. "Scientists do not falsify data. That would be wrong."

6. "Natural selection implies that organisms that are less fit to their environment die. That would be awful! Therefore, natural selection does not exist."

7. "A small amount of marijuana cannot be so bad. Lots of people smoke it."

8. "Darwinists believe that Hitler slaughtered the Jews. Many Christians also believe this. But agreeing with Darwinists would be horrible!"

9. "No professor would be denied tenure just for having a conservative worldview. That would be dishonest."

10. "Morality developed as humans evolved and became dependent upon one another for survival. Hence, it is wrong to murder because this damages society and decreases the chances that individuals within the society will survive and reproduce."

Chapter Review: In this chapter, students should learn how to deal with hypocrisy. Yes, hypocrisy is irrational and immoral. However, hypocrisy does not invalidate an argument. If a hypocrite makes a good argument, then it is a good argument. It is therefore irrational to attempt to refute an argument by pointing out that the person who made it is hypocritical. This may be true, but it is utterly irrelevant.

Likewise, the source of an argument is not relevant to its cogency. An argument is different from a claim. For a claim, it is legitimate to be skeptical of claims that come from a source that has been established to be unreliable. However, an argument stands or falls on its own merit.

Short Answer

For each of the questions below, answer: (A) Is this a genetic fallacy, a *tu quoque* fallacy, or not a fallacy, and (B) why?

1. In a political debate, one candidate says, "My opponent has accused me of mishandling money. This is very ironic considering he himself has been twice investigated for embezzlement."

2. "Capital punishment is a harsh and unenlightened idea. I mean, it comes from the Bible, a book written by primitive goat herders."

3. "Belief in God is a superstitious idea that began when our ancestors were afraid of natural phenomena like lightning. They invented God to comfort them."

4. "The environmentalists make all these arguments that we should save the environment. But they are so wrong. Think about it. They use plastic bags at the grocery store, buy gas-guzzling vehicles, and most of them don't even recycle."

5. "Yes, officer, I may have been speeding. But obviously you were going even faster or you never would have caught me!"

6. "That information comes from the *National Enquirer*, which is known to be unreliable. So I wouldn't accept that claim without support from a more reliable source."

7. "The reason I don't believe in Christianity is because you Christians are such hypocrites. You say one thing, but you do another."

8. "Most of what is supposedly demonstrated in the field of information theory comes from creationists. So their conclusions are probably not very reliable."

Chapter Review: This is a "catch-all" category, because the errors in this section are technically fallacies of irrelevant thesis because they may indeed prove something, but not the point at issue. For example, the strawman fallacy does prove that a particular position is wrong, but it is not the position that the opponent actually holds. When a fallacy of relevance does not fit into any of the above categories, it belongs here. The fallacy of irrelevant thesis is particularly seductive because the conclusion is often true — it just isn't *relevant*.

This fallacy works by distraction. By correctly concluding something that is true (at least potentially), the other person is inclined to agree — without realizing that the topic has been altered. Many arguments get "off track" due to an irrelevant thesis, or a string of them. The goal is for the student to recognize that an argument may indeed prove an issue, but not the issue under discussion. Emphasize to the student that all fallacies of irrelevant thesis can be refuted by this simple response: "True, perhaps, but irrelevant."

Short Answer

For each of the following, answer: Is this the fallacy of irrelevant thesis? Why or why not?

1. "The people who believe in creation are mistaken. Most of them are Christians."

2. Creationist: "Why do you believe in neo-Darwinian evolution?"

   Evolutionist: "Because there is a great deal of scientific evidence in support of it."

3. Teacher: "Jimmy, it appears that you cheated on this exam. What do you have to say for yourself?"

   Jimmy: "It's not like I committed murder or anything."

4. Timothy says, "Dad, why can't I have my own car when I turn 18?"

   Dad responds, "Because Christmas falls on a Friday this year."

5. "The days of creation cannot be ordinary days, because the sun wasn't created until the fourth day."

6. "Christians claim that morality is only justified in the Christian worldview. But I am an atheist, and I am very moral."

7. "Why is it that cars have rear-view mirrors? Clearly, the manufacturer wanted drivers to be able to see what was behind them without turning around."

8. "Why do living creatures have so many complex parts that work together? Because if they didn't, then the animal would have died."

9. "The people who want to reduce the number of guns in the world are mistaken. After all, this will not solve all the world's problems."

10. "Why is it wrong to steal? One man has no authority over another man's property."

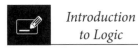
Chapter Review: In a sense, all fallacies of relevance are fallacies of irrelevant thesis. But we reserve that particular fallacy for those fallacies of relevance that do not specifically fall into one of the more specific categories. Therefore, each fallacy of relevance can be answered with this response, "True, perhaps, but irrelevant." We here ask students to identify which fallacy of relevance is committed in the following examples.

Short Answer

For each of the following, identify the fallacy (if there is one) and explain why it is fallacious:

1. "You should not trust any argument that is posted on the Biblical Science Institute website."

2. "You don't need God to account for laws of logic. I don't even believe in God, and I use logic all the time."

3. "You shouldn't believe in or teach creation here; you might get sued."

4. "Clearly, it is not wrong to abort babies. People have been doing it for thousands of years."

5. "If evolution is not true, then why do so many scientists accept it?"

6. "Well, of course Dr. Dave is going to argue for a young earth. He is paid to do that. So you shouldn't accept his argument."

7. "Of course creation cannot be true. Science is limited to the study of the natural world. But creation involves the supernatural."

8. "The Oort cloud clearly must exist. No one has any proof that it doesn't."

9. "Creationists are morons. Do don't be fooled by their arguments."

10. "Creationists do not believe in the scientific method. They simply look to the Bible for all the answers."

Logic Practice Sheets

for Use with

Introduction to Logic

Identify the following fallacies:

1. "Nevertheless, all organisms share some common traits because they all share common ancestors at some point in the past."

2. "You should not trust anything that is posted on the Biblical Science Institute website."

3. "No, evolutionists are not lying about all the evidence for evolution. After all, that would be immoral."

4. "You don't need God to account for laws of logic. I don't even believe in God, and I use logic all the time."

5. "Natural selection tests the combinations of genes represented in the members of a species and encourages the proliferation of those that confer the greatest ability to survive and reproduce."

6. "If you are going to make an argument for creation, you have to use real, mainstream journals, not creationist ones."

7. "You want an example of evolution? You're speaking with one."

8. "Biological evolution refers to changes in the traits of organisms over multiple generations. So creationists are badly mistaken."

9. "The people who want to reduce the number of guns in the world are mistaken. After all, this will not solve all the world's problems."

10. "Why do you deny science?"

Practice Sheet 1 Answers

1. Fallacy of false cause or begging the question. The reason organisms share common traits is the very question at issue. It begs the question to arbitrarily assume that evolution is the reason when that is the point at issue. Furthermore, just because organisms share common traits does not imply that evolution is the cause. So this is a false cause fallacy.

2. Genetic fallacy. The information is arbitrarily dismissed due to its source.

3. Moralistic fallacy. The argument assumes that something does not happen on the basis that it would be unethical.

4. Fallacy of irrelevant thesis. The fact that the atheist can use logic is irrelevant to the issue of whether or not he can *account* for laws of logic on his own worldview, which is the point at issue.

5. Reification fallacy. Natural selection cannot literally "test" or "encourage." If this is part of an argument, then it is a fallacy.

6. No true Scotsman fallacy. The implication is that creationist journals are not "real," yet this goes beyond the dictionary definition of a journal.

7. Begging the question. That people are the result of evolution is the very question at issue. One may not arbitrarily assume such for the sake of proving it.

8. Equivocation fallacy. The argument invokes evolution in the generic sense of change to prove neo-Darwinian evolution, which is quite different.

9. Fallacy of irrelevant thesis. While it is true that a reduction in guns will not solve all the world's problems, this is not the point at issue.

10. Fallacy of complex question. It should be divided into "Do you deny science?" And, "If so, then why?"

Identify the following fallacies:

1. "The ideas supported by creationists, in contrast, are not supported by evidence and are not accepted by the scientific community."

2. "We don't know if birds evolved from the ground up or from the trees down."

3. "Capital punishment is a harsh and unenlightened idea. I mean, it comes from the Bible, a book written by primitive goatherders."

4. "All the classic arguments for God have been refuted. This certainly suggests that God does not exist."

5. "Darwin documented evolution in action by noting how the beaks of finches responded to changes in the environment."

6. "Human beings have an immortal soul. And a finger is part of a human being. Therefore, a finger has an immortal soul, or at least part of a soul."

7. "We are about to enter a century in which the United States will be even more dependent on science and technology than it has been in the past. . . . Yet the teaching of science in the nation's public schools often is marred by a serious omission. Many students receive little or no exposure to the most important concept in modern biology, a concept essential to understanding key aspects of living things — biological evolution."

8. "What is the probability that life could arise by chance? It must be 100 percent because we are here, after all."

9. "If students are taught to simply 'trust in the Bible,' they won't be able to think for themselves, and will not be able to function in society when they grow up."

10. "The only reason you believe in creation is because you are a Christian."

Practice Sheet 2 Answers

1. Faulty appeal to authority. The "scientific community" is invoked as if it were an infallible authority — the standard for all truth claims.

2. Bifurcation fallacy. The third, unstated, and correct option is that birds were created as birds.

3. Genetic fallacy. The argument is dismissed due to its source.

4. Fallacy of appeal to ignorance. Even if the claim were true — that there is no good argument for God — it would not prove that God does not exist.

5. Equivocation fallacy. The "evolution" in beak characteristics does not support evolution in the neo-Darwinian sense of common descent.

6. Fallacy of division. The soul does not divide into the parts of the body.

7. Appeal to emotion or question-begging epithet. No rational argument is given for evolution. Instead, biased language (question-begging epithet) is used to invoke emotions (appeal to emotion) in order to persuade.

8. Begging the question. The way life came about is the very question at issue. The argument arbitrarily assumes evolution as the proof of evolution.

9. Slippery slope fallacy. The action is not likely to set off such a chain of events.

10. Circumstantial *ad hominem* fallacy. The motivation for believing in creation is irrelevant to the truth of creation.

Identify the following fallacies:

1. "Either you use your brain to determine what's true, or you simply accept whatever the Bible says."

2. "The environmentalists make all these arguments that we should save the environment. But they are so wrong. Think about it. They use plastic bags at the grocery store, buy gas-guzzling vehicles, and most them don't even recycle."

3. "Darwinian evolution is easy to demonstrate. The annual changes in influenza viruses and the emergence of bacteria resistant to antibiotics are both products of evolutionary forces."

4. "Do you believe in creation, or do you believe in science?"

5. "God may exist. But we must do science as if He does not. Otherwise, we would never know if we are studying the natural world, or a miracle. Science would come to a standstill."

6. "Human beings cannot have any genuine free will. After all, we are made up entirely of atoms, which have no free will."

7. "An understanding of evolution was essential in the identification of the SARS virus. The genetic material in the virus was similar to that of other viruses because it had evolved from the same ancestor virus."

8. "Nearly all mammals have seven vertebrae in their neck. This is just one of many evidences of the fact that they share a common ancestor."

9. "99.99% of scientists in relevant fields believe in evolution."

10. "Interracial marriage is wrong. You don't see sparrows mating with cardinals."

1. Bifurcation fallacy. The Christian position is that we should use our brain to reason from what the Bible says.

2. *Tu quoque* fallacy. The apparent hypocrisy of the environmentalists does not disprove their argument.

3. Equivocation fallacy. "Evolution" in the sense of changes within a kind as seen in bacteria does not prove evolution in the Darwinian sense of common descent.

4. Bifurcation fallacy. The consistent Christian believes in creation and the methods of science.

5. Slippery slope fallacy. The action is not likely to set off such a chain of events. Miracles are rare by definition, and therefore may be distinguished from natural law by their lack of repeatability.

6. Fallacy of composition. Though the human body is made of parts that have no free will, it does not follow that humans have no free will.

7. Equivocation fallacy. The "evolution" of a virus into the same kind of virus does not remotely support the idea of evolution in the sense that all organisms share a common ancestor.

8. False cause fallacy. That nearly all mammals have seven vertebrae in their neck does not establish that the cause is evolution from a common ancestor.

9. Faulty appeal to authority/majority. That many people believe something does not prove that it is so.

10. Naturalistic fallacy. What happens in nature does not establish what is morally right. Some animals eat their own young, but obviously this is not right for people.

Identify the following fallacies:

1. "I have a very good argument for creation; I know it is sound because every evolutionist I've used the argument on has converted to believing in creation."

2. "Because creationism is based on specific sets of religious convictions, teaching it in science classes would mean imposing a particular religious view on students and thus is unconstitutional, according to several major rulings in federal district courts and the Supreme Court of the United States."

3. "The Oort cloud clearly must exist. No one has any proof that it doesn't."

4. "The arguments of creationists reverse the scientific process. They begin with an explanation that they are unwilling to alter — that supernatural forces have shaped biological or earth systems."

5. "Throughout history, we have consistently found natural explanations for various cosmic and terrestrial phenomena. So, it is reasonable to conclude that the origin of the universe and earth also has a natural cause."

6. "Creationists reject the basic requirements of real science: that hypotheses must be restricted to testable natural explanations."

7. "Evolution is perfectly compatible with God. Scientists and theologians have written eloquently about their awe and wonder at the history of the universe and of life on this planet, explaining that they see no conflict between their faith in God and the evidence for evolution."

8. "My latest book is about the evolution vs. creationism controversy."

9. "People just don't come back to life. Go check out a cemetery. So it just isn't possible for Jesus to have been raised from the dead."

10. "No true American would vote for a Democrat."

Practice Sheet 4 Answers

1. Fallacy of irrelevant thesis. The persuasiveness of an argument does not establish (and is irrelevant to) the soundness of an argument.

2. Special pleading and appeal to force. The appeal to force is the use of legal pressure to prevent the discussion of views contrary to evolution, rather than a logical argument against such views. The argument also commits the fallacy of special pleading because evolution also is based on specific religious convictions (e.g., God either does not exist or used natural forces to shape organisms over time). Yet, evolution is arbitrarily exempted from the claim that religious convictions should not be brought into the science classroom.

3. Fallacy of appeal to ignorance. The lack of proof against a claim is not the same as a proof for the claim.

4. Special pleading. Evolutionists *also* have an explanation that they are unwilling to alter — that natural forces alone are responsible for the universe and life. They have arbitrarily exempted themselves from their own standard.

5. Fallacy of composition or sweeping generalization fallacy. Many of the various parts of the universe may indeed have natural explanations, but that doesn't imply that the universe as a whole has a natural explanation — the fallacy of composition. Alternatively, that most of the universe has natural explanations does not mean that we can assume that there are no exceptions — the sweeping generalization fallacy.

6. No true Scotsman fallacy. The word "real" is prefixed to science to redefine the term such that hypotheses must be restricted to natural explanations. However, the definition of science only requires testability, not *natural* explanations.

7. Faulty appeal to authority. That scientists and theologians think that evolution may be compatible with God is irrelevant to whether evolution is actually compatible with God. An appeal to authority has replaced logical argumentation.

8. Question-begging epithet. A proper comparison would be evolution vs. creation — not creationism. By adding the "ism," the argument implies that creation is merely a belief and that evolution is not, but without making any argument for it. Loaded language is no substitute for logic.

9. Sweeping generalization fallacy. Generally, it is impossible for the dead to be raised. Jesus is an exception because He is God.

10. No true Scotsman fallacy or appeal to emotion. There is nothing in the dictionary definition of "American" that precludes voting for a Democrat. So prefixing "American" with the word "true" merely attempts to protect the claim from counterargument by a rhetorical definition. This could also be classified as the fallacy of the appeal to emotion. Rather than making a logical case, the person attempts to persuade by stirring emotions associated with patriotism.

Identify the following fallacies:

1. "Isn't evolution wonderful? The majesty of the eagle, the incredible speed of the cheetah, the ingenious color-changing ability of the chameleon, and the splendor of a peacock feather are all glorious outcomes of one of nature's most amazing and intricate processes."

2. "Somewhat more than 400 million years ago, some marine plants and animals began one of the greatest of all innovations in evolution — they invaded dry land."

3. "Science tells us that the universe is billions of years old."

4. "Either evolution is true, or everything we know about the world is wrong."

5. "Biblical creation is simply false and unscientific. The Supreme Court has ruled that 'creation science' is a religious idea and that its teaching cannot be mandated in the public schools."

6. Brent has to cancel his date with Emily at the last minute due to a family emergency, so Emily stays home and watches television. Later, Courtney asks Emily, "How was your date with Brent?" Emily says, "I didn't go on a date with Brent." Courtney responds, "Oh, whom did you go with?"

7. "Creationists do not believe in the scientific method. They simply look to the Bible for all the answers."

8. "Are you aware of the fact that evolution has been demonstrated in a laboratory?"

9. "Many teachers are under considerable pressure from policy makers, school administrators, parents, and students to downplay or eliminate the teaching of evolution."

10. "My new theory is better than natural selection because it does not involve the death of the unfit."

1. Appeal to emotion. The statements are intended to stir emotions of appreciation for nature, rather than making a rational argument for evolution. The question-begging epithet is also an acceptable answer since biased language has replaced a rational argument.

2. Reification fallacy. Plants and animals are personified as if part of an army that can "invade." The reification is a fallacy if the statement is part of an argument.

3. Reification fallacy. Science here is personified as if it can say something and is used to draw a conclusion.

4. Bifurcation fallacy. The third unstated and correct option is that evolution is false and we do know some things about the world.

5. Faulty appeal to authority or appeal to fear. What the Supreme Court rules is utterly irrelevant to the truth of any claim, particularly scientific claims. So this is a faulty appeal to authority. It may also be an appeal to fear — that you must not teach creation lest you face legal repercussions.

6. Fallacy of accent. Courtney misunderstood Emily by placing the emphasis on the word "Brent" rather than the word "didn't."

7. Strawman fallacy. Creationists fully embrace the scientific method and would argue that it is based on biblical principles.

8. Fallacy of complex question. The question should be divided: "Has evolution been demonstrated in a laboratory?" And, "If so, are you aware of it?" But since the answer to the first question is "no," the second question isn't meaningful.

9. Appeal to pity. We are supposed to feel sorry for those poor teachers who want to enlighten their students about the truth of evolution, but cannot do so due to legal/political pressure. But no argument for evolution has been made.

10. Appeal to consequences fallacy. That something would be nice doesn't make it true.

Identify the following fallacies:

1. "Creationists reject such scientific facts in part because they do not accept evidence drawn from natural processes that they consider to be at odds with the Bible."

2. "Clearly, it is not wrong to abort babies. People have been doing it for thousands of years."

3. "You cannot travel faster than light. Nature will resist your every effort."

4. "The Bible says that a soft, gentle answer turns away wrath (Proverbs 15:1). But John spoke gently to Henry yesterday, and Henry got angry anyway. So clearly the Bible is wrong."

5. "Life is abundant on earth; almost every possible environment is filled with living organisms. So it is reasonable to conclude that life in space is also quite common."

6. "God does not exist. After all, He kills innocent children; clearly that's not right."

7. "Teaching biology without evolution would be like teaching civics and never mentioning the United States Constitution."

8. "You are really stupid if you believe in creation."

9. "Creationists take the Bible literally. They must believe the earth has corners and pillars. How absurd!"

10. "The Bible states that Noah was to bring two of every animal on board the ark (Genesis 6:19–20). But later it contradicts this by saying that seven of some animals were brought on board (Genesis 7:2)."

1. Strawman fallacy. That creationists reject scientific facts or evidence is simply false and misrepresents the creationist position.

2. Naturalistic fallacy. That something happens does not imply that it is morally right.

3. Reification fallacy. Nature is personified as resisting effort, something it cannot literally do. This is used as part of an argument and is therefore fallacious.

4. Sweeping generalization fallacy. The Proverbs are generalizations — things that are true most of the time. To apply a generalization as if it had no exceptions is the fallacy of the sweeping generalization.

5. Hasty generalization fallacy. The earth is an infinitesimal part of the universe. Hence, experiences on earth are insufficient to extrapolate what happens in the rest of the universe.

6. Fallacy of irrelevant thesis. That God does or allows things that some people don't like is utterly irrelevant to the issue of God's existence.

7. Fallacy of false analogy. Evolution is a belief about how life came to be and is not necessary to understand biology — how life works today, whereas the Constitution is an important aspect of civics.

8. Abusive *ad hominem* fallacy. Name-calling is no substitute for a logical argument.

9. Strawman fallacy. Creationists take the Bible *literarily*, not literally. That is, we take the historical sections as literal, but we embrace the use of non-literal language in poetic sections like the Psalms.

10. Sweeping generalization fallacy. The "two of each kind" is a generalization. The exceptions are those animals of the "clean" kinds which were taken by sevens.

Identify the following fallacies:

1. "The earth's population is roughly 50% male, and 50% female. And you are part of earth's population. Therefore, you are mostly likely 50% male and 50% female."

2. "You are appealing to God, which is a mistake. Science says that we must limit explanations to the natural world."

3. "Given the importance of science in all aspects of modern life, the science curriculum should not be undermined with nonscientific material like creationism."

4. "Creationists are dishonest, so I wouldn't rely on any of their arguments."

5. A coach says to his track team, "If a person runs faster, he can win a race. So, if all of you run faster, you can all win the race."

6. "Evolution by natural selection is not only a historical process — it still operates today. For example, the continual evolution of human pathogens has come to pose one of the most serious public health problems now facing human societies."

7. "Many scientific theories are so well established that no new evidence is likely to alter them substantially. For example, no new evidence will demonstrate that the earth does not orbit around the sun (heliocentric theory). . . . Like these other foundational scientific theories, the theory of evolution is supported by so many observations and confirming experiments."

8. "For example, evidence for a very young earth is incompatible with many different methods of establishing the age of rocks."

9. "No one should doubt the truth of evolution. The scientific consensus around evolution is overwhelming."

10. "In the future, we expect that nature will be uniform because it has been that way in the past."

Practice Sheet 7 Answers

1. Fallacy of division. Gender is binary characteristic that does not divide from a group of people to individuals.

2. Reification fallacy. Science doesn't literally "say" anything, but is personified here as part of an argument.

3. Question-begging epithet. The main error here is the use of biased language in substitution for a rational argument. Namely, creation is dismissed as "nonscientific" without any argument.

4. Abusive *ad hominem* fallacy. The argument of the creationists is dismissed by attacking the character of the persons.

5. Fallacy of composition. Only one person can win a race.

6. Equivocation fallacy. Evolution in the sense of common-ancestry is being argued by giving an example of change within a kind — an entirely different type of "evolution."

7. Fallacy of false analogy. The heliocentric solar system can be verified by experiments in the present. Neo-Darwinian evolution cannot.

8. Begging the question. The methods by which rocks are dated assume evolutionary notions, such as uniformitarianism and naturalism. Therefore, to use such methods to prove evolutionary notions begs the question.

9. Faulty appeal to authority/majority. That the majority of scientists believe something does not make it true.

10. Begging the question. Uniformity is the idea that the future will be like the past in terms of basic principles. So, to assume that there will be uniformity in the future merely on the basis that there has been uniformity in the past is to assume that the future will be like the past — uniformity. The arguer has arbitrarily assumed uniformity as the basis for proving uniformity.

Identify the following fallacies:

1. "Either you live by faith, or you have rational reasons for what you believe."

2. "The synapses of the brain must have at least some degree of consciousness, since the brain is made up of these synapses and is conscious."

3. "I realize that evolution from single-celled organisms to people by mutations and natural selection may seem unlikely. But it is obviously true because we are here."

4. "What is the mechanism by which birds evolved their wings?"

5. "The universe is both alive and not alive, because it is made up of both living and non-living things."

6. "Even a casual look at different kinds of organisms reveals striking similarities among species, and anatomists have discovered that these similarities are more than skin deep. All vertebrates, for example, from fish to humans, have a common body plan characterized by a segmented body and a hollow main nerve cord along the back. The best available scientific explanation for these common structures is that all vertebrates are descended from a common ancestor species and that they have diverged through evolution."

7. "Creationists try to find answers in the Bible, but real scientists do research to find out what happened in the past."

8. "Japan has the second highest percentage of atheists. And it has one of the lowest crime rates in the world. Clearly atheism is good for society."

9. "Scientists have looked at the arguments [for creation] and have found they are not supported by verifiable data."

10. "The scientific position is evolution. Creation is just religious nonsense."

1. Bifurcation fallacy. We should live by faith and have rational reasons for our beliefs. Our faith in the Bible has very good reasons.

2. Fallacy of division. Just because the brain has consciousness does not mean that the parts of the brain have parts of consciousness.

3. Begging the question or fallacy of irrelevant thesis. That we are here is true but irrelevant to the question of how we got here. To arbitrarily assume that we got here by evolution for the sake of proving evolution is to beg the question.

4. Fallacy of the complex question. The question should be divided: "Did birds evolve their wings?" And, "If so, what was the mechanism?" Since the answer to the first question is "no," the second question is unnecessary.

5. Fallacy of composition and fallacy of contradiction. That parts of the universe are alive (or not alive) does not mean that the universe as a whole is alive (or not alive). Furthermore, the notion that the universe is alive and not alive at the same time in the same sense violates the law of non-contradiction.

6. Fallacy of false cause or begging the question. The cause of such similarity is falsely attributed to evolution. The argument arbitrarily assumes that evolution is the cause, which is the very topic at issue.

7. No true Scotsman fallacy and strawman fallacy. That "real" scientists supposedly do not look to the Bible is not part of the definition of a scientist — hence the no true Scotsman fallacy. Furthermore, while creationists do try to find answers in the Bible, we also do other kinds of research to understand past events.

8. False cause fallacy — the *cum hoc ergo propter hoc*. The unproven assumption is that atheism has caused the crime rates to be lower, merely on the basis that they go together.

9. Faulty appeal to authority. The argument neglects to mention that many scientists do find the arguments for creation to be supported by verifiable data.

10. Question-begging epithet. Loaded language is used to persuade, not a rational argument.

Identify the following fallacies:

1. "If Genesis is true, then why is there so much evidence for an old earth?"

2. "To deny that evolution takes place would be like denying the existence of gravity."

3. "You shouldn't believe in or teach creation here; you might get sued."

4. "Scientific conclusions [like evolution] are not limited to direct observation but often depend on inferences that are made by applying reason to observations." [On the same page, in explaining why creation is not science]: "But science cannot test supernatural possibilities. . . . Because such appeals to the supernatural are not testable using the rules and processes of scientific inquiry, they cannot be a part of science."

5. "Well, of course Dr. Dave is going to argue for a young earth. He believes in creation. So you shouldn't accept his argument."

6. "Indeed, U.S. courts have ruled that ideas of creation science are religious views and cannot be taught when evolution is taught."

7. "The bones in the forelimbs of terrestrial and some aquatic vertebrates are remarkably similar because they have all evolved from the forelimbs of a common ancestor."

8. "Evolution is a scientific fact; virtually all the top scientists believe in it."

9. "We accept evolution as the best scientific explanation for a lot of observations — about fossils and biochemistry and evolutionary changes we can actually see, like how bacteria become resistant to certain medicines."

10. "Because the evidence supporting it is so strong, scientists no longer question whether biological evolution has occurred and is continuing to occur."

Practice Sheet 9 Answers

1. Fallacy of complex question. The question should be divided: "Is there evidence for an old earth?" And, "If so, how can that be if Genesis is true?" Since the answer to the first question is "no," the second question is unnecessary.

2. Fallacy of false analogy. Gravity is testable and repeatable in the present, but particles-to-people evolution is not.

3. Appeal to fear/force. Rather than making a rational argument against creation, the threat of legal action is used to persuade.

4. Fallacy of special pleading. The last part of the quote argues against creation on the basis that it is not directly testable. But the first sentence attempts to exempt evolution from this principle.

5. Circumstantial *ad hominem* fallacy. The beliefs or motivations of the person are irrelevant to the soundness of his argument.

6. Fallacy of irrelevant thesis or appeal to fear/force. What U.S. courts have ruled to be legal or illegal is irrelevant to what is true. However, the threat of legal action might be used in place of an argument to persuade.

7. Fallacy of false cause. Similarity does not imply that the cause is evolution. Some cars have certain features in common, but they are not biologically descended from a common ancestor.

8. Faulty appeal to authority. That many scientists believe something about the past doesn't make it so.

9. Equivocation fallacy. The changes observed within bacteria are "evolution" of a sort but do not establish evolution in the particles-to-people sense.

10. Question-begging epithet and faulty appeal to authority. Biased language asserting strong evidence is used instead of a rational argument to persuade — the question begging epithet. The arguer has appealed to scientists rather than presenting any actual scientific evidence — the faulty appeal to authority.

Identify the following fallacies:

1. "No, you can't have another dog. If I were to get you another dog, then pretty soon, you'd want another, and then another. And we cannot handle a house full of dogs!"

2. "Evolution is an inescapable fact. Everything in the universe, from stars and galaxies to finch beaks and bacteria, is in a constant state of evolution."

3. "My cousin got this chain letter in the mail, but he didn't forward it on. Two weeks later, he had a fatal heart attack. Don't tell me chain letters don't do anything!"

4. "Look, pirating movies from the Internet can't be wrong. Everyone does it."

5. "The earth must be billions of years old because we find fossils that are at least billions of years old."

6. "Evolution is no longer questioned in science. . . . One of the most characteristic features of science is this openness to challenge. The willingness to abandon a currently accepted belief when a new, better one is proposed is an important demarcation between science and religious dogma."

7. "Furthermore, many key aspects of evolution occur in relatively short periods that can be observed directly — such as the evolution in bacteria of resistance to antibiotics."

8. "The atomic structure of matter, the genetic basis of heredity, the circulation of blood, gravitation and planetary motion, and the process of biological evolution by natural selection are just a few examples of a very large number of scientific explanations that have been overwhelmingly substantiated."

9. "Why are creationists against scientific progress?"

10. "If students are not taught evolution, they will not understand how science really works, and will be deprived of a proper understanding of nature."

Practice Sheet 10 Answers

1. Slippery slope fallacy. The suggested action is not likely to set off the chain of events that are claimed.

2. Equivocation fallacy. The argument attempts to prove evolution in the neo-Darwin sense by giving examples of other types of change, which are irrelevant to Darwinian evolution.

3. False cause fallacy — the *post hoc ergo propter hoc*. Just because one event happened after another does not mean that the one event caused the other.

4. Naturalistic fallacy. What people actually do is not relevant to what people should or should not do.

5. Begging the question. That fossils are billions of years old is an evolutionary assumption; to argue that it proves evolution is to assume the point at issue.

6. Special pleading or contradiction. The argument asserts that the key to science is its openness to challenge, while simultaneously asserting that evolution is no longer questioned and therefore not open to challenge. This is a contradiction. The arguer dismisses creation on the basis that it is supposedly not open to challenge, while exempting his own belief in evolution from this same criterion — special pleading.

7. Equivocation fallacy. The "evolution" of bacteria to resist antibiotics is a change within a kind; this does not in any way prove evolution in the sense of all kinds sharing a common ancestor.

8. Fallacy of false analogy. The arguer attempts to establish the credibility of evolution by listing it among many legitimate branches of science. But unlike all these other sciences, particles-to-people evolution cannot be observed or tested in the present.

9. Fallacy of complex question. The question should be divided: "Are creationists against scientific progress?" And, "If so, why?" But the answer to the first question is "no," and therefore the second question is unnecessary.

10. Slippery slope fallacy. The stated action is not likely in reality to set off the chain of events that are claimed.

Logic Quizzes and Final Exam

for Use with

Introduction to Logic

Fill in the blank: (10 points each)

1. _____ is the study of the principles of correct reasoning. It is the way God thinks.

2. To be _____ is to reason incorrectly. But God, by His nature, always reasons correctly.

3. Unbelievers too are made in the image of God, and hence have the capacity for _____ reasoning. God has given them knowledge as well.

4. The Bible reveals that human beings are made in God's image, and therefore reflect some of His attributes, including the ability to _____.

5. God always thinks correctly, and the Bible commands us to think like Him (Isaiah 55:7–8) and emulate His _____ (Ephesians 5:1).

6. A _____ is a truth claim. It is the meaning of a statement and is always either true or false.

7. An _____ is a series of propositions in which the truth of one is said to follow from the others.

8. A good argument has true _____, and the conclusion follows from them.

9. The _____ is the opposite of a given proposition. It is formed by adding "It is not the case that" to the original proposition. It always has the opposite truth value of a given proposition.

10. _____ is having confidence (or proof, or good reasons) for what you have not experienced with your senses. It is a confident expectation in that which is unseen (Hebrews 11:1).

Fill in the blank: (10 points each)

1. To be _____ is to not have a specific reason for a belief or action: not having a reason.

2. A _____ definition is the meaning of a word as listed in a dictionary.

3. A _____definition is consistent with the definition of a word found in a dictionary, but adds further restrictions for the purpose of clarification.

4. A _____ is a (categorical) argument with two premises and one conclusion that uses words like "all, some, no, not."

5. A logical _____ is a common error in reasoning.

For the following arguments, identify the premise(s) and the conclusion: (10 points each)

6. You really should go to church since the Bible tells you to in Hebrews 10:25.

7. We really shouldn't murder because it violates God's law.

For the following enthymemes, supply the unstated proposition to make the argument valid: (10 points each)

8. All basketball players are very tall.
    Therefore, all Celtics are very tall.

9. All men are mortal.
    Socrates is a man.

10. Natural selection does not literally select anything.
    Therefore, it is not really real.

Identify the specific fallacy of ambiguity in the following claims. Answers may include: equivocation fallacy, reification fallacy, fallacy of accent, fallacy of division, and the fallacy of composition. (10 points each)

1. "Science tells us that the universe is billions of years old."

2. "Biological evolution refers to changes in the traits of organisms over multiple generations. So creationists are badly mistaken."

3. Brent has to cancel his date with Emily at the last minute due to a family emergency, so Emily stays home and watches television. Later, Courtney asks Emily, "How was your date with Brent?" Emily says, "I didn't go on a date with Brent." Courtney responds, "Oh, whom did you go with?"

4. "Evolution is an inescapable fact. Everything in the universe, from stars and galaxies to finch beaks and bacteria, is in a constant state of evolution."

5. "Human beings cannot have any genuine free will. After all, we are made up entirely of atoms, which have no free will."

6. "The synapses of the brain must have at least some degree of consciousness, since the brain is made up of these synapses and is conscious."

7. A coach says to his track team, "If a person runs faster, he can win a race. So, if all of you run faster, you can all win the race."

8. "We accept evolution as the best scientific explanation for a lot of observations — about fossils and biochemistry and evolutionary changes we can actually see, like how bacteria become resistant to certain medicines."

9. "Sorry Samantha, you can't join our club. The sign says 'no girls.'" Samantha responds, "I know it says no girls — plural. But I'm not girls — plural, I'm a girl. So you can have one."

10. "What force created all the intricate parts of organisms, as well as the magnificent features on earth? Is it some 'creator'? No. It is time. Time designs organisms, builds mountains, and moves continents."

For each of the following, identify the specific fallacy of presumption. Answers may include: the hasty generalization fallacy, sweeping generalization fallacy, the false cause fallacy, begging the question, question-begging epithet, complex question, bifurcation fallacy, no true Scotsman fallacy, false analogy, and the slippery slope fallacy. (10 points each)

1. "Japan has the second highest percentage of atheists. And it has one of the lowest crime rates in the world. Clearly atheism is good for society."

2. "Do you believe in creation, or do you believe in science?"

3. "The scientific position is evolution. Creation is just religious nonsense."

4. "Creationists reject the basic requirements of real science: that hypotheses must be restricted to testable natural explanations."

5. "If Genesis is true, then why is there so much evidence for an old earth?"

6. "What is the probability that life could arise by chance? It must be 100 percent because we are here, after all."

7. "People just don't come back to life. Go check out a cemetery. So it just isn't possible for Jesus to have been raised from the dead."

8. "To deny that evolution takes place would be like denying the existence of gravity."

9. "Life is abundant on earth; almost every possible environment is filled with living organisms. So it is reasonable to conclude that life in space is also quite common."

10. "If students are taught to simply 'trust in the Bible,' they won't be able to think for themselves, and will not be able to function in society when they grow up."

For each of the following, identify the specific fallacy of relevance. Answers may include: faulty appeal to authority or majority, strawman fallacy, appeal to emotion, appeal to pity, appeal to fear/force, naturalistic fallacy, moralistic fallacy, appeal to consequences, *tu quoque* fallacy, and the fallacy of irrelevant thesis. (10 points each)

1. "My new theory is more likely to be true than natural selection because it does not involve the death of the unfit."

2. "Evolution is perfectly compatible with God. Scientists and theologians have written eloquently about their awe and wonder at the history of the universe and of life on this planet, explaining that they see no conflict between their faith in God and the evidence for evolution."

3. "God does not exist. After all, He kills innocent children; clearly that's not right."

4. "You shouldn't believe in or teach creation here; you might get sued."

5. "Look, pirating movies from the Internet can't be wrong. Everyone does it."

6. "Creationists reject such scientific facts in part because they do not accept evidence drawn from natural processes that they consider to be at odds with the Bible."

7. "Isn't evolution wonderful? The majesty of the eagle, the incredible speed of the cheetah, the ingenious color-changing ability of the chameleon, and the splendor of a peacock feather are all glorious outcomes of one of nature's most amazing and intricate processes."

8. "Many teachers are under considerable pressure from policy makers, school administrators, parents, and students to downplay or eliminate the teaching of evolution."

9. "The environmentalists make all these arguments that we should save the environment. But they are so wrong. Think about it. They use plastic bags at the grocery store, buy gas-guzzling vehicles, and most them don't even recycle."

10. "No, evolutionists are not lying about all the evidence for evolution. After all, that would be immoral."

Choose from the following regarding the argument being stated: (5 points each)

Sweeping generalization fallacy	Question-begging epithet	Strawman fallacy
Bifurcation fallacy	Fallacy of composition	No true Scotsman fallacy
Tu quoque fallacy	Special pleading	Begging the question
Naturalistic fallacy	Fallacy of accent	Faulty appeal to authority
Fallacy of division	Fallacy of complex question	Reification fallacy
Moralistic fallacy	Fallacy of irrelevant thesis	Appeal to consequences fallacy
False cause fallacy	Faulty appeal to authority	

1. "No, evolutionists are not lying about all the evidence for evolution. After all, that would be immoral."

2. "If you are going to make an argument for creation, you have to use real, mainstream journals, not creationist ones."

3. "Why do you deny science?"

4. "The ideas supported by creationists, in contrast, are not supported by evidence and are not accepted by the scientific community."

5. "Human beings have an immortal soul. And a finger is part of a human being. Therefore, a finger has an immortal soul, or at least part of a soul."

6. "What is the probability that life could arise by chance? It must be 100 percent because we are here, after all."

7. "Either you use your brain to determine what's true, or you simply accept whatever the Bible says."

8. "The environmentalists make all these arguments that we should save the environment. But they are so wrong. Think about it. They use plastic bags at the grocery store, buy gas-guzzling vehicles, and most them don't even recycle."

9. "Human beings cannot have any genuine free will. After all, we are made up entirely of atoms, which have no free will."

10. "Nearly all mammals have seven vertebrae in their neck. This is just one of many evidences of the fact that they share a common ancestor."

11. "Interracial marriage is wrong. You don't see sparrows mating with cardinals."

12. "I have a very good argument for creation; I know it is sound because every evolutionist I've used the argument on has converted to believing in creation."

13. "The arguments of creationists reverse the scientific process. They begin with an explanation that they are unwilling to alter — that supernatural forces have shaped biological or earth systems."

14. "Evolution is perfectly compatible with God. Scientists and theologians have written eloquently about their awe and wonder at the history of the universe and of life on this planet, explaining that they see no conflict between their faith in God and the evidence for evolution."

15. "My latest book is about the evolution vs. creationism controversy."

16. "People just don't come back to life. Go check out a cemetery. So it just isn't possible for Jesus to have been raised from the dead."

17. "Somewhat more than 400 million years ago, some marine plants and animals began one of the greatest of all innovations in evolution — they invaded dry land."

18. Brent has to cancel his date with Emily at the last minute due to a family emergency, so Emily stays home and watches television. Later, Courtney asks Emily, "How was your date with Brent?" Emily says, "I didn't go on a date with Brent." Courtney responds, "Oh, whom did you go with?"

19. "Creationists reject such scientific facts in part because they do not accept evidence drawn from natural processes that they consider to be at odds with the Bible."

20. "My new theory is better than natural selection because it does not involve the death of the unfit."

Logic Answer Keys

for Use with

Introduction to Logic

Worksheet Answers

Chapter 1: Logic and the Christian Worldview

1. Logic is (the study of) the principles of correct reasoning. Some students may answer that logic is the study of the way God thinks. I suggest giving full credit for this answer as it is a true statement and an important point in the chapter; but gently remind them that the *definition* of logic (as found in a dictionary) is the study of the principles of correct reasoning.

2. Several possible answers here. God is the standard by which all reasoning should be judged to be correct or incorrect because His mind determines truth. To study logic is to study how God thinks.

3. Yes. Atheism is a belief about God. As such, it is inherently religious.

4. Many possible answers. Moral questions, mathematical truths, spiritual questions, most historical questions. Accept any question that (1) can be answered, but (2) cannot be demonstrated to be true by observation and experimentation.

   Examples:

   Is it wrong to murder?

   Is infinity real?

   What happens to the soul after death?

   Who was the first president of the constitutional United States of America?

5. No, God cannot say something false. There are several good answers as to why He cannot:

   (A) What God says determines reality. (B) It is contrary to God's self-consistent nature. (C) The universe becomes whatever God says.

   Some students may be bothered that God cannot do some things. Does this conflict with the notion that God is all-powerful? No. God being all-powerful means that He can do anything He pleases — anything that is consistent with His nature. It does not please God to lie, and it is not consistent with His nature to do so.

6. No. God cannot learn anything new because He already knows everything. There is no knowledge beyond God's mind. God's mind is the source of all truth.

7. We can think in a way that is self-consistent / logical. Other possible answers: We can think truthfully. We can use laws of logic. We can consider abstract ideas. We can use math. We can make moral judgments.

8. Many possible answers: We can be mistaken. We can learn new things. We can violate laws of logic. We can be illogical. We can believe something that is false. We cannot think outside of time. We cannot consider all the infinite possibilities. We cannot know everything. We cannot be sure of all our conclusions.

9. Our mind ___discovers___ truth.

   God's mind ___determines___ truth.

   [This question emphasizes one of the differences between God's mind and ours. God is the giver of knowledge; we are the receivers.]

10. No, God cannot be illogical. To be illogical is to reason incorrectly. But God, by His nature, always reasons correctly. To be illogical is to think differently from God; but God cannot think differently from God because He is God.

Chapter 2: All Knowledge Is Ultimately from God

1. Knowledge ultimately comes from God. He is the original source of all knowledge. We know this because God Himself has told us so in His Word — the Bible.

2. Revelation is the giving of knowledge. In this context, it is God giving knowledge to man.

3. Special revelation is the Bible: God's Word. It is that aspect of God's revelation that is written in human language, and as such is objective and propositional.

4. Objective means "outside the person" and therefore not subject to the person's mind, feelings or opinions. Things which are objective are the same for all people. This stands in contrast to subjective things like feelings or opinions that can differ from person to person.

5. Propositional means "made up of meaningful sentences" (in a human language). Technically, it means made up of propositions, but the students have not yet learned that term. Propositional knowledge has a special clarity to it because it is made up of words.

6. Several possible answers:

   Some knowledge is built into us directly by God, such as God's moral law.

   Some knowledge is gained by sensory experience: using our eyes, ears, and other senses to probe the outside world.

Some knowledge is gained through rational deduction and inward contemplation using our God-given mind.

Some knowledge is given by communication in language, such as God's special revelation, or things learned from teachers and parents.

7. Several answers are possible. We can be rational. We have the ability to analyze arguments, to distinguish truth from falsehood, to reason. We are aware of ourselves and others. We have knowledge of right and wrong. We can make judgments. God also does all these things.

8. God's mind is infinite, but our mind is finite. God knows everything; we do not. Our mind works within time; we draw conclusions after reasoning through the premises, but God's mind is beyond time. Our mind has the capacity to learn new truths, but God's mind already knows all truths. God's mind determines truth, whereas our mind discovers truth. God's mind is the source of all knowledge; our mind is the recipient of some. God's mind cannot be mistaken, but ours can be.

9. They too are made in the image of God, and hence have the capacity for rational reasoning.

God has given them knowledge as well. (You might emphasize that this is an example of "common grace" — the theological principle that God gives some good things to everyone.)

They learn by the same God-given senses and mind that Christians use, but unbelievers are not grateful to God nor do they give Him thanks (Romans 1:21).

10. No. They still must use the mind that God gave them. They still use the sensory organs that God designed for them. They are still made in the image of God, even if they deny these things. It would be ridiculous to assume that a non-designed "brain" that formed by accident would necessarily be capable of rational thought. Therefore, unbelievers are tacitly relying on the Christian worldview when they reason about anything. This shows that they do know about God's existence, but they suppress that truth in unrighteousness (Romans 1:18).

Chapter 3: Why Study Logic?
1. Several possible answers: (A) The Bible reveals that human beings are made in God's image, and therefore reflect some of His attributes, including the ability to reason. (B) God commands us to do so; and God would not give a command that is impossible for us to follow.

2. God always thinks correctly, and the Bible commands us to think like Him (Isaiah 55:7–8) and emulate His character (Ephesians 5:1).

3. We are more likely to have true beliefs if we think logically, which will better enable us to function in this world. We will be less likely to be fooled by a bad argument if we understand logic. Right reasoning will help us understand science, mathematics, ethics, history, language, and just about any other topic.

4. Man's basic problem is that his thoughts and ways are not God's thoughts and ways; man does not think or behave in a way that is consistent with God's character.

5. The solution is repentance: man must turn from his sinful thoughts and ways and learn to think and behave according to God's nature.

6. Many possible answers here. Considering that we are commanded to make disciples of all nations, we should argue for the Christian faith when there is an opportunity to help someone become a disciple. First Peter 3:15 suggests that when a person asks you about your faith, why it is you believe what you believe, and the person is apparently sincere, then a defense of the faith is appropriate.

7. Many possible answers here. One example would be a situation where someone is clearly not interested in listening, not open to reason, and only wants to argue. The Bible indicates that we should not cast our pearls before swine. Sometimes a person seems to be sincere at first, but becomes angry and hostile when presented with a defense of Christianity. There is likely nothing to be gained by continued conversation with a person who has such an attitude. There are many pragmatic answers as well: during the middle of a battle, when performing brain surgery, in the middle of a church sermon, etc.

8. Many possible answers here. The chapter itself indicated that the belief that gravity is not real will likely lead to disaster. The belief that people are bulletproof, the belief that we do not need water or oxygen to live, the belief that we do not need to look both ways before we cross the street, the belief that unborn babies are not actually human, all these will likely have a disastrous outcome. False moral beliefs can also lead to disaster: the belief that it is okay to murder people, the belief that theft is not wrong, the belief that rape is not wrong, and so on.

9. We cannot think <u>exactly</u> like God because He is infinite and we are finite. But it is possible to think in a way that is consistent with His character. If it were not possible to think in a way that is consistent with God's thinking, then God would not have commanded us to do so, as He does in Isaiah 55:7–8.

10. Logic can be considered an aspect of theology because logic is the study of the way God thinks. By definition, logic is the study of correct reasoning, but God's thinking defines what constitutes correct. Therefore, to study logic is to study something about the mind of God.

Chapter 4: Propositions and Arguments

1. Logic is the study of the principles of correct reasoning. It is the way God thinks.

2. An argument is a series of propositions in which the truth of one is said to follow from the others.

3. (1) It has true premises, and (2) the conclusion follows from them.

4. Yes. It is either true or false. The truth value may be hard to determine and somewhat subjective depending on the speaker, but it has one.

5. Yes. It has a truth value, albeit one that is subjective and depends on the preferences of the speaker.

6. No. Questions are not propositions. They have no truth value.

7. No. Requests and commands are not propositions. They have no truth value.

8. Yes. This claim is either true or false. Note that no human knows what the truth value of this proposition is. But it must have one due to the nature of the claim. Therefore, it is a proposition. This question tests the student's ability to recognize that the claim has a truth value (and is therefore a proposition) without knowing what that truth value is.

9. Yes. False propositions are still propositions. If the student responds with a "no," remind him or her that propositions do not have to be true. A proposition is simply a claim. It will have a truth value that is either true or false.

10. No. Commands are not propositions.

11. No. Questions are not propositions.

12. Yes. The truth value may be true or false depending on the speaker.

13. Yes. This has a truth value, though it may be subjective (depends on who says it).

14. (A) Yes, it is an argument with two premises and a conclusion.

    (B) Yes, it is reasonable. The premises are true, and the conclusion follows from them.

15. (A) No. A single proposition cannot be an argument. An argument must have a conclusion and at least one premise.

16. (A) Yes. The conclusion "you should believe in evolution" is based on the premise "Most scientists believe in Darwinian evolution."

    (B) No. Just because a lot of people (even educated people) believe in something doesn't necessarily mean that you should.

17. (A) Yes, two premises and one conclusion.

    (B) Yes, the conclusion follows from the premises, and the premises are true.

18. (A) No. Questions are not propositions, and therefore not part of an argument.

    This question examines the student's ability to recognize that the word "since" does not always imply a premise of an argument.

Chapter 5: Inductive and Deductive Reasoning

1. Inductive. The conclusion is likely; but it is not guaranteed by the premise. That is, even if the premise is true, the conclusion could be false. The word "probably" in the conclusion gives this away.

2. Deductive. The conclusion is definitely true if the premises are.

3. Deductive. The conclusion is definitely true if the premises are.

4. Inductive. The conclusion is likely; but it is not guaranteed since Dr. Lisle might have other reasons for not answering the phone. The phrase "most likely" in the conclusion reveals that this is inductive.

5. Deductive. The conclusion would definitely be true if the premises were true. In this case, the first premise is false. But the conclusion definitely follows from the premises — so deductive. This example shows that inductive/deductive is about whether the argument claims to be definitive or merely likely, not whether the argument has true premises.

6. Inductive. There are other causes of lung cancer besides smoking. Non-smokers can also get lung cancer, though it is less likely than for smokers.

7. Premise: Republicans better represent Christian values. (Note the premise indicator word "because.")

   Conclusion: You should vote for Republicans.

8. Premise: The Bible tells you to go to church. (Note the premise indicator word "since.")

   Conclusion: You really should go to church.

9. Premise: Murder violates God's law. (Note the premise indicator word "because.")

   Conclusion: We shouldn't murder.

10. Premise 1: My new dog is a golden retriever. (This is a premise because it is obvious from observation.)

    Premise 2: Most golden retrievers have a pleasant demeanor. (Note the premise indicator word "since.")

    Conclusion: My new dog will probably have a pleasant demeanor. (Note the conclusion indicator word "so.")

    Also, note that this is an example of an argument where the conclusion is in the middle; it is preceded and followed by a premise.

11. Premise: All organisms are based on DNA.

    Conclusion: They have descended from a common ancestor. (Note the conclusion indicator word "therefore.")

    Note that the conclusion does not actually follow from the premise; so, this is a bad argument.

12. Premise: All the medical doctors say that smoking causes cancer.

    Conclusion: We know that smoking causes cancer. / Smoking causes cancer.

    Note that there are no indicator words in the premise or conclusion. But context clearly indicates that the claim "all medical doctors say so" is being used to support the conclusion that "smoking causes cancer."

13. Premise: They [all vertebrate animals] all have certain anatomical similarities.

    Conclusion: [no doubt] All vertebrate animals share a common ancestor.

    This is another example of an argument with no indicator words for the premise or conclusion. The student must think through what the person is trying to prove — the conclusion, and what statement is provided as support for the conclusion.

It is also an example of bad argument because many things have similarities without being descended from a common ancestor.

14. Premise: Stars look very tiny.

    Conclusion: Stars are very far away. (Note the phrase "must be" indicates reasoning toward a conclusion. In other words, given the premise that stars look tiny, the conclusion "must be" that they are far away.)

Chapter 6: The Biblical Basis for the Laws of Logic

1. It is not the case that all dogs are black. (Some students may answer: "No dogs are black" or "All dogs are not black." These are wrong answers because they are *not equivalent* in meaning to the actual negation. "It is not the case that all dogs are black" is consistent with the possibility that some dogs are black, just not all of them. Be sure to point out the distinction. A negation may have an alternate wording besides "It is not the case that . . ." but only as long as it has the same meaning. "Some dogs are not black" is very close to the negation, except that the former has existential import [it linguistically implies that dogs exist] while the actual negation does not. This caveat goes beyond what is covered in this text.)

2. It is not the case that water is wet. (In this case, "water is not wet" or "water is dry" might be a suitable alternative. But the safest way to ensure a negation is to simply add "It is not the case that. . . .")

3. It is not the case that blue is my favorite color, or Blue is not my favorite color. (Answers such as "red is my favorite color" are not negations. They may be incompatible with the original proposition, but they are not the negation of it.)

4. Law of identity. (what Pilate wrote is what Pilate wrote.)

5. Law of the excluded middle. (Either you are for Christ or against [not for] Him. Granted, "against" may be stronger than merely "not for." So Christ has gone beyond merely the excluded middle to make the point that there is no neutral position in regards to Himself. But this is still based on the law of the excluded middle.)

6. Law of non-contradiction. (Paul affirms that his word is not contradictory: it is not yes and no. It is not yes and not-yes.)

7. Law of excluded middle. Either it is appropriate to

pay taxes, or it is not the case that it is appropriate to pay taxes.

8. Law of identity. Those upon whom God has mercy/compassion are those upon whom God has mercy/compassion.

9. Law of non-contradiction. (The saying is "you can't have your cake and eat it too" — "eating it" implies that you no longer have it. So you can't have your cake and also <u>not</u> have it. The statement above denies this, and therefore violates the law of non-contradiction.)

10. Law of the excluded middle. (It has to be one or the other. Either p [to be] or not-p [not to be]. By saying, "neither," the person violates this law.)

11. Law of non-contradiction. (It cannot be the case that p [my car is in the garage] and not-p at the same time. The speaker violates the rule.)

12. Law of identity. (Everything is itself.)

Chapter 7: Logical Failure of the Unbiblical Worldview

1. God is omnipresent and upholds all things by the word of His power; therefore, laws of logic will work everywhere since God's mind controls the entire universe. (I suggest accepting any answer that references God's omnipresence, God's sovereignty, or the fact that God upholds the entire universe.)

2. God is beyond time and does not change. God Himself is invariant. Hence, His thoughts are invariant and do not change with time. An alternative answer, also correct, is that God is faithful.

3. First, laws of logic do not describe the physical universe; that is not what they are about. Rather, laws of logic describe the correct chain of reasoning from premises to conclusion. Second, the physical universe is different in different locations and at different times. So, laws of logic would change from place to place and from time to time if they merely reflected the physical universe.

4. Allah is not self-consistent. The Quran, supposedly the revelation of Allah, both endorses and denies the Gospel of Jesus. So, clearly Allah cannot be the basis for the law of non-contradiction since he denies what he also affirms. An alternative correct answer is that Allah does not exist as a real god, and a non-existent god cannot be a rational basis for anything.

5. No. First, no polytheistic worldview can make sense of one universal standard of reasoning. Different gods would have different ways of reasoning, and so there would be many contradictory sets of laws of logic, not just the one. Second, the Greek gods are not omnipresent, and are within time. Therefore, they cannot account for the universal and invariant nature of laws of logic.

6. No. Laws of logic existed before people (two contradictory propositions could not both be true, even if there were no people around to verify it). Laws of logic are universal, but people are not. Laws of logic do not change with time, but manmade laws do change with time.

7. No. A fictional god cannot be the basis for anything because that which is real cannot rest on that which is unreal. Just as a real house cannot rest on an imaginary foundation, the real laws of logic cannot rest or owe their existence to something unreal.

8. No. Several possible answers here. (1) A god that people invented would not exist before people, and therefore cannot make sense of the fact that laws of logic existed before people. (2) A god that people invented would be imaginary and cannot therefore be responsible for anything that is real, like laws of logic. (3) An invented god would necessarily be different from the living God, and only the living God can justify the laws of logic.

9. No. Several possible answers here. (1) If the flying spaghetti monster were identical to the biblical God in every way, then it would have the same name, and would therefore not be called "the flying spaghetti monster." So the premise is self-refuting. (2) How could anyone know the characteristics of the flying spaghetti monster, to see if such characteristics are in fact identical to God? We know God's characteristics due to His revelation in the Bible. But the flying spaghetti monster has no similar objective revelation.

10. No, the reasoning is not correct. It is fallacious to arbitrarily assume that something will be in the future as it was in the past. After all, I have never died in the past, but it would be silly to conclude: "Therefore, I will never die in the future." Many things change over time, and the unbeliever has no rational basis for assuming that his past experience with logic will apply in all future situations. The problem is essentially this: human experience is extremely limited. It is limited to the near past, and pretty much to earth. Yet people assume that

logic applies at all times, past and future, and throughout the universe. But only God is in a position to know this, and He has revealed so in His Word. Only the Christian position can make sense of our confidence that laws of logic apply at all times in all locations.

Chapter 8: Is the Christian Faith Illogical?

1. Something is intuitive if it makes sense to you, if it matches your feelings or expectations. Something is logical if it aligns with the way God thinks, if it involves correct reasoning from true premises.

2. Many possible answers: anywhere someone in the Bible quotes someone saying something that is not true. Examples: The Bible records that Peter said he would not deny Christ (Matthew 26:35), but he did deny Christ (Matthew 26:74). The serpent said to Eve that she would not die (Genesis 3:5), which was not true (Genesis 2:17).

3. Lots of possible answers: Pray for those who despitefully use and persecute you (Matthew 5:44). Bless those who curse you (Luke 6:28). The meek shall inherit the earth (Matthew 5:5). You are blessed when you have been insulted/persecuted for righteousness (Matthew 5:10–11). Whoever exalts himself shall be humbled, but he who humbles himself shall be exalted (Matthew 23:12). No one is good except God (Luke 18:19).

4. It is not a contradiction because is one in a different sense than He is three. A contradiction requires p and not-p in the same sense. God is one in essence, but three in persons.

5. The law of non-contradiction. This is a behavioral inconsistency because their behavior reveals that they think it is indeed okay to make arguments, but they verbally profess the negation. Essentially they are saying p and not-p (it is okay and not okay to make arguments).

6. Possible answers: (A) God cannot deny Himself, and the Bible is His Word. Therefore, the Bible cannot contradict in anything it affirms. (B) The Bible is true, and truth cannot contradict truth.

Chapter 9: Is Faith Contrary to Reason?

1. Faith is having confidence (or proof, or good reasons) for what you have not experienced with your senses. It is a confident expectation in that which is unseen (Hebrews 11:1).

2. It is logical to have faith in God. Many good reasons can be given. First, any alternative to God leads to absurdity. Apart from God we could never justify our expectation that the universe is orderly and will continue to be so in the future, or that our senses are basically reliable. Another good answer would be that God knows everything, is never mistaken, and never lies, so of course it is logical to trust in Him. It would be illogical to not have faith in God.

3. It is *not* logical to rely on emotions as a basis for truth because emotions are notoriously unpredictable, constantly changing, and do not necessarily have a connection to truth.

4. The heart refers to the essential core of the person. It is the mind of man — the seat of man's intellect / reasoning / thoughts (Genesis 6:5; Psalm 14:1).

5. There is no contradiction because 1 Corinthians 1:21 is not referring to genuine foolishness, but rather what the secular world considers to be foolish, which is in fact actually wise: the preaching of the Gospel. Nothing the Bible affirms can contradict anything else the Bible affirms, since the Bible is God's Word and God cannot deny Himself.

6. Unbelievers may have limited "pockets" of wisdom on non-spiritual matters. For example, they may save some of their financial earnings for the future, which is fiscally wise. They may decide to refrain from doing illegal drugs or committing murder; these are wise decisions. However, they are able to do this only because God has extended some grace to them as well. After all, unbelievers do know God (in an unsaved way — Romans 1:18–20), but are not grateful for His grace. However, unbelievers do not have wisdom in an ultimate sense, or on spiritual issues. They do not have wisdom in regard to salvation. Those who reject God's offers of grace and mercy are foolish (Psalm 14:1).

7. To be rational, you must have a good reason (or several good reasons) for your beliefs, and this must be consistent with your other reasons and beliefs.

8. Our sensory organs were designed by God (Proverbs 20:12), who is not the author of confusion (1 Corinthians 14:33), but is the Truth (John 14:6). (This may be a good place to remind students that, due to sin, our senses are not always perfectly reliable. Blindness and other disease might render senses useless, but these would not have been in existence before sin. And God has given

us other senses as checks in case one or two of our sensory organs are damaged.)

9. God upholds creation by His power (Hebrews 1:3) and is a God of order, not confusion (1 Corinthians 14:33). God has promised us that the basic cycles of nature will be in the future as they have been in the past (Genesis 8:22).

Chapter 10: Arbitrariness and Inconsistency

1. Arbitrariness (not having a reason), and inconsistency (holding mutually contrary claims). (The answer is stated directly in the second paragraph of the chapter.)

2. To be arbitrary is to not have a specific reason for a belief or action: not having a reason.

3. No, there is nothing in Scripture or laws of logic that requires personal preferences to have a specific reason behind them. It is no sin to have a favorite color without having a specific reason for it. Any personal preferences that are matters of opinion rather than fact are examples: "Classical music is better than Jazz. Dogs are great! Cats are not good pets. I like pizza." None of these require justification. However, factual claims should not be arbitrary, because their truthfulness is not determined by our preferences. Arbitrariness in logical reasoning is to be avoided because it leads to unreliable conclusions.

4. [Many examples are possible]
"I don't think I need Jesus for salvation; I think God will let me in to heaven since I'm basically a good person." The belief that basically good people go to heaven is asserted but not justified.
"I just bought a lottery ticket, and I think I'm going to win this time!" There is no reason to justify such a belief.
"I think all religions are true." This is not only arbitrary, but also inconsistent since different religions make contrary claims.

5. The chapter specifically mentions *contradictions* and *behavioral inconsistency* (hypocrisy) as two types often committed. (However, the student may offer specific examples instead.)

6. By the law of non-contradiction, a claim which contains two contradictory claims is always false. Thus, inconsistent reasoning will lead to unreliable conclusions.
[alternatively]
Inconsistency is a type of lie and is morally

unacceptable.
[alternatively]
God does not deny Himself, therefore, we should be self-consistent to honor Him.

7. By refuting arbitrariness with arbitrariness, the absurdity of the critic's position is exposed. He cannot refute my arbitrary claim without admitting that arbitrariness is unacceptable.

8. Refuting inconsistency with inconsistency reveals the absurdity of the critic's line of reasoning. The critic cannot refute a contradictory claim without admitting that contradictions are unacceptable in logic.

9. Yes. God does not deny Himself (2 Timothy 2:13). And we are to emulate God's character (Ephesians 5:1; Isaiah 55:7–8). And we are to take captive every thought into obedience to Christ (2 Corinthians 10:5). Therefore, we have a moral obligation to be consistent in our thinking.

10. (Any example where a person's words do not match his or her actions.)
A person claims that racism is wrong but refuses to talk or engage with people that have a different skin color from his own.
A person claims that murder is wrong but is for abortion.

Chapter 11: Definitions

1. This is a precising definition because it is consistent with the dictionary but adds additional constraints (which are reasonable) for the purpose of clarification; that is, a Ph.D. is not necessarily required to be a scientist. But this qualification may help for the purposes of doing a statistical study.

2. A lexical definition is that which is found in a dictionary.

3. This is a persuasive/rhetorical definition. It is not found in any dictionary and is therefore a false definition that is being used to influence the opinions of the reader.

4. This is a theoretical definition because it goes along with the theory that black holes exist and have a region inside in which nothing can escape the pull of gravity.

5. This is a stipulative definition. When carbon-60 was discovered, its discoverers were free to stipulate its name. The term has since become lexical since it is now found in a dictionary.

6. This is a precising definition. The definition is found in a dictionary but is restricted to only one of the lexical definitions for the purpose of discussion.

Chapter 12: A Brief Introduction to Syllogisms

1. No. A sound argument is one that is *valid* and has true premises. Therefore, an invalid argument is always unsound.

2. Yes. A valid argument with a false premise is unsound. Many examples are possible; however, the conclusion must follow from the premises:

   All dogs can fly. Spot is a dog. Therefore, Spot can fly.

   Some cats are dogs. All cats can purr. Therefore, some dogs can purr.

3. Subject term: Celtics

   Predicate term: things that are very tall (or very tall things/people)

   Middle term: basketball players

   All B are T

   All C are B

   Therefore, All C are T

   (Note that the students are free to assign different letters, so long as the form is the same.)

4. Subject term: Texans

   Predicate term: football players

   Middle term: Dallas Cowboys

   All D are F

   Some T are D

   Therefore, some T are F

5. Subject term: aquatic creatures

   Predicate term: things that have lungs

   Middle term: fish

   No F are L

   Some A are F

   Therefore, some A are not L

6. Invalid. Both premises are true, but the conclusion does not follow from them. Since it is invalid, it is automatically unsound.

7. Valid and sound. The premises are both true and the conclusion follows necessarily from them.

8. Valid but unsound. The first premise is false;

therefore, the argument is unsound. However, the structure is correct. If the first premise were true, then the conclusion would follow necessarily.

9. Invalid and unsound. All the propositions here are true, but the conclusion does not follow from the premises. To see that it does not, simply substitute "cats" for "bats" in this argument. The first two premises would still be true, and yet the conclusion is false. Hence, the form of the argument is faulty, and invalid. Since it is invalid, it is automatically unsound. Point out to the students that even though every proposition in this argument is true, it is still invalid and unsound because the structure is wrong.

10. Valid and sound. The premises are both true and the conclusion follows necessarily from them.

Chapter 13: Enthymemes

1. The unstated premise is the conclusion: "Therefore, Dr. Dawkins believes in evolution."

2. The unstated minor premise is: "This insect has bulbs at the tip of its antennae."

3. The unstated major premise is: "All things that have a misleading name do not exist" or "All things that have a misleading name are things that do not exist."

4. [Note that this argument is not in standard order. The conclusion is stated first, followed by a paraphrase of the minor premise (Tim is a Christian).]
   The unstated major premise is: All Christians are creationists.

5. The unstated major premise is: "Things that (in my opinion) are very mean do not exist."

6. The unstated conclusion is: "Therefore, it will probably be clear tonight."

7. The unstated major premise is: "That which is non-literal is not really real" or "That which does not literally select anything is not really real."

8. (Again, the argument is not in standard form. The conclusion is stated first "you should tithe" or "tithing is something you should do" followed by the (paraphrased) minor premise "tithing is something that Bible commands of you.")
   The unstated major premise is "All that the Bible commands are things you should do" or more colloquially, "You should do what the Bible says you should."

9. The unstated conclusion is "Therefore, this will make you stronger."

10. The unstated minor premise is "Kenny is a scientist with a Ph.D."

Chapter 14: Informal Logical Fallacies

1. Fallacy of presumption.

2. Fallacy of relevance.

3. Fallacy of ambiguity.

4. Fallacy of presumption. The argument assumes without evidence that negative remarks about a Democrat prove that a person is a Republican.

5. Fallacy of ambiguity. The argument confuses "evolution" in the sense of generic chance, with Darwinian evolution — a particular model of origins.

6. Fallacy of relevance. Joe's unwillingness to (or exemption from) paying taxes is not relevant to his claims or arguments regarding government.

7. Fallacy of presumption. The arguer has tacitly assumed without proof that all scientists believe in evolution.

8. Fallacy of ambiguity. The word "practice" is used in two different senses without due notice of the change: "practice" in the sense of doing something repeatedly with an effort to improve, and the medical practice.

Chapter 15: Equivocation

1. (A) Yes, this is an equivocation fallacy. (B) The term "science" is used in the sense of the scientific method in the first proposition, and in the sense of a particular model/hypothesis in the second, which is a very different meaning. It does not follow logically that because we accept the method of science as a powerful tool for answering certain questions, that we must embrace any particular hypothesis.

2. (A) No. There is no fallacy here because the word "doctor" is used in the same sense in both premises.

3. (A) No. The term "evolution" (unstated in the second proposition) is used in the same sense in both propositions — the sense of common descent. So there is no fallacy.

4. (A) Yes, this is an equivocation fallacy. (B) The term "evolution" is used in two different senses. The conclusion that creationists are badly mistaken is based partly on the premise that evolution is a scientific fact. Here, "evolution" must refer to Darwinian (particles-to-people) evolution, since this is the type of change that creationists deny. However, the second premise uses the term "evolution" in the sense of change within a kind — which creationists accept.

5. (A) Yes, this is an equivocation fallacy. (B) The equivocated term is "interpretation." In the sense of interpreting the Bible, it means to understand the meaning of propositional statements. However, in the sense of interpreting nature, it means to create propositional statements from our observations. These two different meanings of "interpretation" are conflated as if they were the same type of thing.

6. (A) Yes, this is an equivocation fallacy. (B) The equivocated term is "science" which is used in the sense of operational science in the first premise, but refers to a particular view of origins science in the second.

7. (A) No fallacy here. The term "science" is used in the same sense in both propositions.

8. (A) Yes, this is a classic example of equivocation. (B) The word "evolution" is used in the sense of change within a kind in the first propositions, but then is switched to mean Darwinian evolution later without notice of the change.

9. (A) There is no fallacy here. The word "Christian" is used consistently.

10. (A) This is an equivocation fallacy, and a rather subtle one. (B) The word "omnipotent" is used in two different ways. In the first premise, it means that God can do anything He pleases — anything that is consistent with His nature. However, in the conclusion, "omnipotent" is used to mean anything whatsoever, even logical absurdities (God is truth and therefore cannot lie).

Chapter 16: Reification

1. This is reification because nature does not have a mind or senses such that it can search for a way, and therefore cannot literally find a way. It is fallacious because it is used as part of a logical argument: as a solution to a potential problem.

2. This is reification because life is described poetically as invading the land, as if it were an army about to conquer an enemy. But land is not a literal enemy to be conquered, nor do amphibians possess such a military mindset. The reification is not necessarily

fallacious, because this is not necessarily part of an argument. It may simply be a poetic way of telling the evolutionary story.

3. This is reification because natural selection is the name given to the observation that organisms better suited to their environment tend to survive better than those that don't. It cannot literally guide development. This is a fallacious use of reification because it is part of an argument and uses poetry to obscure the problem of how mindless processes can supposedly design organisms.

4. This is a classic example of reification because science cannot literally say anything. It is certainly a fallacy because it is used as part of an argument, to supposedly prove that you should not appeal to God.

5. This is reification because fossils don't literally say anything at all. It is not fallacious because it is simply a book title and not part of an argument. Book titles often wax poetic.

6. This is reification because nature does not literally have a mind that it can have plans. However, it is not fallacious because it is not part of an argument. It is a poetic way of indicating that the picnic was cancelled due to unpleasant weather.

7. This is a mild use of reification since evolution (in the Darwinian sense) is a concept and cannot literally tell anything. Of course, "tell" can also be used in a poetic way, as in "time will tell." This reification is fallacious because it is being used as part of an argument.

8. This is reification because science here is said to be atheistic, but science is not a person such that it can have the belief that God does not exist (or any other belief). This is fallacious because it is used as part of an argument — the "because" gives it away.

9. This is not reification. Scientists are people and can literally know things. (Of course, I would argue that scientists actually know that life is the creation of God.) So, the argument is faulty, but it is *not* the fallacy of reification.

10. This is reification. Evidence does not literally lead anywhere. Rather, scientists draw conclusions based on their understanding of the evidence. There is insufficient context to determine whether this is part of an argument. Therefore, either answer from the student should be acceptable. However, it seems to be part of an argument attempting to persuade the person to draw a different conclusion

from the evidence, in which case it is a fallacious use of reification.

Chapter 17: The Fallacy of Accent

1. Equivocation fallacy. The word "light" is used in the first proposition to mean "not heavy." But in the second proposition the meaning is changed and light is used to mean "electromagnetic radiation." The conclusion is therefore fallacious.

2. Fallacy of accent. Tammy has inferred undue emphasis on the word "I" as in "*I* didn't get groceries on Monday." She falsely concludes that Stacy meant to indicate that groceries were bought, just not by Stacy.

3. Equivocation fallacy. In the first premise "man" means humankind, but in the second premise it refers to one of the two sexes. The conclusion is therefore unreliable.

4. Reification fallacy. Nature is an abstract concept meaning everything that happens. It doesn't literally resist us, as if it had a mind and will. The reification is part of an argument and is being used to draw a conclusion. It is therefore fallacious.

5. Courtney has committed the fallacy of accent by placing undue emphasis on the word "Brent." Namely, she assumes that Emily meant to imply "I didn't go on a date with *Brent*" (but rather with someone else).

6. This is reification, and since it is being used to draw a conclusion it can be considered fallacious (though perhaps only mildly since the meaning is pretty clear). Fairness is not a person that can literally demand anything.

7. Pat has committed the fallacy of accent in falsely assuming that Terry had emphasized the phrase "behind their back" — as if that is the real objection rather than bad talk in general.

8. Troy has committed the fallacy of accent in emphasizing the word "her," as if Paul really is sure that he is in love, just not necessarily with Amy. Most likely the word Paul is emphasizing is actually "love." So the issue is not about which person Paul likes, but rather whether his feelings toward Amy are really love.

9. This is an equivocation fallacy. The term "headache" is used in the first proposition somewhat non-literally. Namely, rambunctious children are not actually a headache, but are rather the cause of the headache. But in the second

proposition, the term "headache" refers to a literal headache. The meaning has switched.

10. This is reification. The concept of religion is treated as if it were a person that can deceive and kill. Whether it is considered a fallacy or a legitimate use of reification depends on whether this is viewed as a poetic statement, or part of an argument. Only context will determine that. (Therefore, some students may view it as legitimate reification, other students may view it as a fallacy. Either answer is acceptable given the lack of context.)

Chapter 18: The Fallacies of Composition and Division

1. This is the fallacy of composition. The conclusion — that the (whole) airplane cannot fly — is based on the illicit assumption that this property transfers from the parts. But "flying" is not a property of nature; it is an emergent phenomenon for certain machines that are comprised of non-flying parts.

2. This is the fallacy of composition. I know that a lot of creationists use this argument. And there may be a modified version of the argument that avoids this fallacy. But stated this way, it is not obvious that causality *within* the universe extends to causes *of* the universe.

3. This is a classic example of the fallacy of composition. The argument confuses the distributive "all" with the collective "all." An individual bus uses more gas than a car, but collectively all cars use more gasoline than all buses.

4. This is the fallacy of division. The soul is an aspect of an entire person and cannot be divided as such. So, the fact that a human being has a soul does not mean that any given part of a human being has a soul or part of a soul.

5. This is the fallacy of composition. The fact that the person likes the taste of two different things does not imply that the person will like the taste of the combination of those things. Taste is a property that does not transfer between the whole and the separate ingredients.

6. This is the fallacy of composition. Life is not a property that transfers from non-living parts to a living whole.

7. This isn't really a fallacy so much as a misunderstanding. Renae falsely assumes that Tim is using the collective "all" rather than the distributive "all." In other words, she has assumed

that Tim means that there is at least one person who has contracted and survived every type of cancer. But really Tim simply meant that for any one type of cancer, there are some people who have survived it.

8. This is the fallacy of composition. The coach has taken a principle that is true in a distributive sense (if an individual runs faster, he or she is more likely to win), and applied it collectively (if everyone runs faster, then everyone will be more likely to win). But this doesn't transfer because if everyone runs faster then there will still be only one winner.

9. This is a legitimate division. There is no fallacy here because obedience to natural law transfers between the whole and the parts.

10. This is the fallacy of division. Although the brain is the seat of consciousness, it is not the case that part of the brain is partly conscious. Consciousness is not a property that divides into parts.

Chapter 19: Hasty Generalization and Sweeping Generalization

1. This is a sweeping generalization fallacy. The generalization is that two of each animal was to be brought aboard; but God specifies an exception to this — 7 (or perhaps seven pairs) of each clean kind is to be brought on board. Actually, this isn't so much an exception as an addition, since 7 animals includes the 2, and then 5 more.

2. This is a hasty generalization fallacy. The fact that one school experienced this trend is not sufficient to establish that this is generally the case. One example is never enough to establish any generalization.

3. This is a sweeping generalization fallacy. The Proverbs are generalizations, not exceptionless rules. But this critic has falsely assumed that the trends recorded in Proverbs are exceptionless.

4. This is a hasty generalization fallacy. The fact that one pair of sisters look alike is not sufficient to establish that this is generally the case. Remember, one instance of anything is not sufficient to reliably establish a generalization.

5. This is a hasty generalization fallacy. The fact that similarities in DNA in some cases correlate with biological descent does not establish that this is generally true. DNA similarities within a kind may be indicative of the closeness of relations, but this does not automatically extend to DNA similarities

between kinds.

6. Brenda has committed the sweeping generalization fallacy. The right to freedom of speech is a generalization and it does have exceptions. One of those exceptions is yelling "fire" in a movie theater when there is no fire.

7. This is a hasty generalization fallacy. A mere three examples out of the 4 billion women on the planet is not sufficient to establish that women, in general, cannot be trusted.

8. This not a fallacy. It is a legitimate inference. (Even if students don't know much about Los Angeles, they have no reason to suspect that it is an exception to a very reasonable generalization.)

9. This is not a fallacy. The generalization is well justified because we have thousands of observations of the motions of the 8 planets and thousands of asteroids that all validate Kepler's laws.

10. This is a sweeping generalization fallacy. The generalization that people cannot walk on water is well justified by the scientific method. However, it has an exception: Jesus. Jesus is not bound by the laws of nature.

Chapter 20: The Fallacy of False Cause

1. This is a false cause fallacy, specifically, the *post hoc ergo propter hoc*. The arguer has fallacious assumed that the beating of the drums caused the sun to return merely because the latter happened after the former. But the sun would have returned anyway, regardless of the beating of any drums.

2. This is a false cause fallacy, specifically, the *post hoc ergo propter hoc*. The arguer fallaciously concludes that the shooting was a result of the new policy merely on the basis that it happened afterward.

3. There is no fallacy here. Since studying does tend to result in higher scores, it is reasonable to assume that Jim's studying was at least partly the cause of his higher score. Of course, this is not conclusive, but inductive arguments don't have to be conclusive, only reasonable.

4. There is no fallacy here. "Whenever" implies that the person has had several instances of this, and the stomach pain always follows after eating dairy products. So, it is reasonable to assume that the succession is necessary, and lactose intolerance is a reasonable explanation, though not conclusive.

5. This is a false cause fallacy, of the *post hoc*

ergo propter hoc kind. There may indeed be a causal connection between the cooling of the environment and the fact that the animals now have thicker fur. But the explanation that they have self-adjusted is not supported by evidence. It may be that some animals already had thicker fur and were well-suited to survival and reproduction as the environment got cold, whereas the ones that didn't died. Perhaps no individual animal did any self-adjusting, but merely the relative proportions changed. In any case, there is insufficient data for the person to draw the conclusion that he did.

6. This is a false cause fallacy. It is a *cum hoc ergo propter hoc*. Just because humans and apes have similarities in their anatomy does not establish the cause of that similarity.

7. This is a false cause fallacy. It is *cum hoc ergo propter hoc* since the claim is made that atheism goes along with lower crime rates, and therefore must be the cause. Even if the premises are true, we have insufficient information to conclude that atheism is the cause of the lower crime rates. There are many other factors that would have to be eliminated.

8. This is legitimate reasoning, not a fallacy. When the book is placed on the board, the board stops vibrating. The wording "whenever" suggests that the person has performed the experiment many times with the same result. This suggests that the succession is necessary. Putting the book on the board causes the board to stop vibrating. (Note that the person doesn't need to understand the details of the mechanism, nor the cause of the board vibrating in the first place. He has shown that the succession is very likely necessary, which is all that is needed for his conclusion to be justified.)

9. This is a classic *post hoc ergo propter hoc* fallacy. The person has assumed that breaking the chain has caused his cousin's misfortune when there is no logical basis for this.

10. This is legitimate reasoning, not a fallacy. "Whenever" implies that the experiment has been tried many times. When the aspirin is not taken, the headache continues. But when the aspirin is taken, the headache stops. Hence, we have good evidence of causation.

Chapter 21: Begging the Question

1. This begs the question because the conclusion that evolution must be true is based on the premise that it is a well-established fact, which is just another

way of saying it is true.

2. This begs the question because the methods of science and induction are based upon the premise that the past experiences can be used to predict future outcomes. Yet this is the very thing the arguer has assumed when he argues that we can have confidence in science and induction (in the future) because they have worked in the past. That confidence would only be justified if past experience can be used to predict future outcomes, the very thing the arguer is being asked to justify.

(This is an extremely important point. Be prepared to discuss this in some depth with the students.)

3. This does not beg the question. The claim that the moon shines by reflected sunlight is defended by appealing to something else, not itself. There is no fallacy here.

4. This begs the question because the way in which we got here is the very point at issue. The arguer has simply assumed that evolution is the way we got here, as the sole support for his claim that evolution is true. That life came about by evolution is the very claim at issue, and one may not simply assume it for the sake of proving it.

5. This does not beg the question. The arguer does not assume creation is true as the sole reason for believing it but appeals to other reasons for support.

6. This begs the question. (This is the spatial equivalent of the problem of justifying how the future will be like the past. In this case, we are asking how we know that "over there" will be like "here.") Unless we already knew some other way that deep space is like the earth in some ways, we could not argue that deep space will be like earth just because different places on earth are like each other. The argument arbitrarily assumes the very thing it attempts to prove.

7. This begs the question because the arguer has tacitly assumed that the supernatural is impossible, which is really the claim at issue. Biblical creation is supernatural. And therefore to arbitrarily dismiss the supernatural is to arbitrarily dismiss creation — the very thing the person is supposed to be arguing against.

8. This begs the question because the fact that God does not lie is recorded in the Bible, and the truth of the Bible is the very claim at issue. (Point out to the students that both claims are true: The Bible is indeed true. God indeed cannot lie. However, the

fact that each statement is used as the sole support for the other is fallacious.) The fact that the same argument could be used to "prove" the contrary claim in the next example shows it is a fallacy.

9. This begs the question because the claim at issue is whether the Quran is the Word of God, which we must not arbitrarily assume for the sake of proving it.

10. This begs the question because the entire point of producing evidence for evolution would be to establish that it is a fact, which is what the arguer has arbitrarily assumed.

Chapter 22: Begging the Question — Part 2

1. This is virtuous. Any attempt to argue against words would have to use them. They are not arbitrary.

2. Vicious/fallacious. The arguer has arbitrarily assumed that creation is the reason we are here, which is the very point at issue.

3. This is virtuous. Though it uses logic, any alleged refutation would have to use logic as well.

4. Vicious/fallacious. The arguer has arbitrarily assumed that laws of logic will work tomorrow and that we will be able to reason tomorrow. But this is not necessary in order to reason today. The alternative would <u>not</u> be self-refuting.

5. This is virtuous. Any attempt to argue that God is dishonest would necessarily assume that our mind and senses are reliable as if designed by an honest God.

6. Vicious/fallacious. The arguer has arbitrarily assumed what he is supposed to be proving — that the way we got here is the big bang.

7. Vicious/fallacious. This error is seductive because it may seem reasonable that organisms with unreliable senses would be weeded out. However, most organisms have no senses at all: grass, trees, etc., and yet continue to thrive. The arguer has arbitrarily assumed that he is not grass or a tree because he has sensory experiences that he believes to be reliable — the very thing he is attempting to prove.

8. Vicious/fallacious. In assuming that the rock layers were deposited gradually, the arguer has tacitly assumed that they were not deposited rapidly during the biblical flood. That is, he has arbitrarily rejected biblical history, and then concludes that

the Bible is wrong — the very assumption he started with.

9. Vicious/fallacies. This is one of the most common fallacies in debates on the issue of induction. We grant that the laws of nature worked in the past. But when the arguer says, "Therefore, in the future it will be that way" he has tacitly assumed that past experiences are indicative of future success. But that would only be true if the laws of nature continue in the future as they did in the past. The arguer has arbitrarily assumed his own conclusion in order to draw his conclusion.

10. This is virtuous. Whether pro-air or anti-air, anyone wanting to make an argument for or against the existence of air would have to use air to make it. Thus, it is reasonable to believe in air. The alternative would make argumentation impossible; and yet argumentation is possible.

Chapter 23: The Question-Begging Epithet

1. This is a question-begging epithet, and a very subtle one. The suffix "ism" has been attached to creation but not to evolution. Since "ism" implies a belief, this subtly suggests that creation is merely a belief whereas evolution is a fact. But this has not been established logically. It is mere rhetoric. The more objective way to frame the debate would be "evolution vs. creation" or alternatively "evolutionism vs. creationism."

2. This is a question-begging epithet because it implies that there is a conflict between creation and science when this has not been established. In fact, biblical creation is the necessary precondition for science as explained in the book *The Ultimate Proof of Creation*. Or perhaps, the arguer means to imply that evolution (the alternative to creation) is science whereas creation is not. But no argument has been made. The more objective way to frame the debate would be "creation versus evolution."

3. There is no fallacy here. The person is making a claim, and will attempt to make a rational argument supporting it. The argument may or may not contain fallacies — we won't know until he makes it. But there is no problem stating the thing to be demonstrated first.

4. This is a question-begging epithet because biased language ("obviously wrong") is used in place of a rational argument. The correct way to state this is "Creation is wrong because of the following reasons: _____." Of course, he will not have good

reasons. But at least the claim will no longer be so biased.

5. Vulgar language is always a question-begging epithet. It has no other purpose than to stir an emotional response. The only way to fix this is to not use vulgar language and replace it with a rational argument.

6. This is a question-begging epithet because the person has made no argument, but merely used biased language ("religious nonsense") to persuade someone of an unproved position. A way to fix this is to replace it with a rational argument, showing scientific support for evolution. Of course, I would say that this cannot be done.

7. This quote by Richard Dawkins is a question-begging epithet because it smuggles in Dawkins' belief that God doesn't exist using biased language ("fiction") instead of a rational argument. The way to fix it would be to attempt a rational argument against God's existence. But this cannot be done because to make any argument presupposes God's existence.

8. This is not a fallacy. Although I would be skeptical that the person could make good on his claim, he is not using biased language in place of a rational argument — not yet anyway.

9. This is a question-begging epithet because rather than making a logical case against creation, the person has merely used biased language to imply that intelligent people don't believe in creation. That's not a rational argument. Rather than saying "because I'm intelligent," the person should have said, "for the following reasons: _____" and then supplied an actual argument. Of course, the argument won't be a good one since he is arguing against something that is true. But at least he will then have made an actual argument, and not merely used biased language.

10. This is a question-begging epithet because it uses biased language rather than logic to imply that faith in creation is "blind" and that evolution is the more enlightened position. Furthermore, it implies that evolution is not a blind faith, but provides no support. The only way to salvage this mess would be to replace the entire thing with a rational argument that fairly compares and contrasts faith in evolution with faith in creation. "I believe it makes more sense to have faith in evolution than in creation for the following reasons: _____." The reasons could then be analyzed. At the very least, the person could

state his position without such bias, even though he presents no argument: "I used to believe in biblical creation, but now I believe in evolution."

Chapter 24: The Complex Question

1. A. Does all the evidence point to evolution?
   B. If so, how can that be the case if creation is true?

2. A. Does the world look old?
   B. If so, how can that be the case if it is really young?

3. A. Are creationists against science?
   B. If so, why?

4. A. Has evolution been demonstrated in a laboratory?
   B. If so, are you aware of it?

5. A. Did life arise from random chemicals and diversify into all the species we see on earth today?
   B. If so, how?

6. A. Are scientists able to probe the distant past, and learn what life was like millions of years ago?
   B. If so, how?

7. A. Do you believe in nonsense and reject science?
   B. If so, are you going to stop?

8. A. Are creationists ignorant of the facts?
   B. If so, why?

9. A. Did birds evolve wings?
   B. If so, what is the mechanism?

10. A. Is evolution important to our understanding of biology?
    B. If so, why?

Chapter 25: The Bifurcation Fallacy

1. This is a bifurcation fallacy. The third alternative is that evolution is false, and we do know some things about the world.

2. This if a bifurcation fallacy. (Be sure to spend some time on this one. It is extremely common and based on an incorrect understanding of what faith is. Many people think that faith is when you believe something without having reasons. But this is contrary to the biblical definition of faith. Biblical faith is rational — we have good reasons to believe that God is who He claims to be in His Word.) The third alternative is something like this: "I have good reasons for my faith in God."

3. This if a bifurcation fallacy because creation is not contrary to rationality. In fact, it's required. The third

alternative is: "I am a creationist and I am rational." Or "I am a creationist because I am rational."

4. There is no fallacy here. This claim is true by the law of the excluded middle since belief in God is contradictory to atheism. There is no third alternative.

5. This is a bifurcation fallacy because natural laws are not contrary to the upholding power of God. In fact, laws of nature <u>are</u> the upholding power of God. That is, natural laws are descriptions of the way God normally upholds His creation.

6. This is a bifurcation fallacy because there are other possibilities. Perhaps it is morning and there is dew on the ground, yet with no rain. Perhaps someone just dumped a bucket of water on the ground. There are many possibilities.

7. There is no fallacy here. This is true by the law of the excluded middle. Since the two positions are contradictory, one of them must be true and the other false. There is no third alternative.

8. This is a bifurcation fallacy because the primary way the Holy Spirit tells us what to do is through the text of the Bible. The Holy Spirit inspired the text of the Bible (2 Peter 1:21). A possible third alternative is "I listen to the Holy Spirit to tell me what to do, all the things He has told me in the text of the Bible."

9. This is a bifurcation fallacy — and a very common one. The third alternative is "God is in control of everything that happens, including our free choices." That may be difficult to understand, but it is *not contradictory*. The freedom to choose means that within certain limits, we can do as we please. But then again, God can control what pleases us (Proverbs 21:1). So our free choices are not contrary to His control, but in fact result from it. Everything that comes to pass is part of God's plan (Isaiah 46:9–11).

10. This is a bifurcation fallacy. The third alternative is "Those who disbelieve Darwinian evolution are actually very well informed, and generally quite honest."

Chapter 26: The No True Scotsman Fallacy

1. "Yes, but no *true* dog is black." (Any similar answer will do. Exact wording need not match.) Alternatively, "Yes, but Spot is not *truly* black."

2. "They are not *real* scientists. *Real* scientists don't believe the Bible."

3. "Ah, but no *legitimate*/*real* technical journals publish creationist articles." / "No *serious* technical journals publish creationist articles."

4. "But no *genuine* Christian believes in evolution."

5. "Ah, but *true* faith is blind."

6. This is not a fallacy because a scientist is defined as someone who does science, which entails following the scientific method. This is a legitimate use of the definition.

7. This is a no true Scotsman fallacy. Although it is terribly inconsistent for a Christian to embrace evolution, the definition of "Christian" is someone who follows Christ. The definition says nothing about evolution. Of course, people who follow Christ consistently will reject evolution; but not all Christians are consistent.

8. There is no fallacy here. The term "real" is being used for emphasis. It is not being used to redefine "evidence" so as to protect the claim from counterargument.

9. This is a no true Scotsman fallacy because there is nothing in the definition of "scholar" that requires one to dismiss the historical information contained in the Bible.

10. This is a no true Scotsman fallacy because there is nothing in the definition of "American" that has anything to do with how a person *votes*.

Chapter 27: Special Pleading

1. This is special pleading. John's reason for wanting to exempt himself from the law is not one that the Bible itself specifies. He is being arbitrary.

2. This is not a fallacy. A pastor preaching on a Sunday is something the Bible endorses, and therefore is a biblically justified exception to the general principle that a person should rest on that day. There are a few other exceptions listed in Scripture as well.

3. This is special pleading. Being late is not a legally justified exception to the law against speeding.

4. This is not necessarily fallacious. A medical emergency may well be a legitimately recognized exemption to laws against speeding.

5. This is special pleading. An evolutionist generally requires that other truth claims be supported by evidence, but he has arbitrarily exempted evolution from this requirement.

6. This is special pleading. (This is a classic example that occurs often!) The Bible is itself an ancient historical document. To arbitrarily dismiss its history just because it's the Bible is without any rational merit.

7. This is not a fallacy. Laws of nature describe the normal, predictable operation of the universe, not miracles. Miracles are — by definition — unusual. So, their exemption is justified.

8. This is special pleading because the creation of the universe in six days was also a miracle. Jeff accepts one miracle recorded in Scripture but arbitrarily rejects another.

9. This is special pleading because the person making the claim is imposing his morality on other people by making the statement about what they should not do. He is doing what he says you should not do (hypocrisy) without giving any reason why he should be exempt from the rule.

10. This is special pleading because the articles of the Biblical Science Institute are peer-reviewed. Yet, this person has arbitrarily decided that they do not count. Such an arbitrary exception is what makes special pleading a fallacy.

Chapter 28: The False Analogy and the Slippery Slope Fallacy

1. This is a slippery slope fallacy. It is unlikely that teaching creation will result in the claimed series of events because science presupposes that God upholds the present universe in a consistent way that the mind can discover.

2. This is a false analogy. Cars do not reproduce. Organisms do. Evolution is supposed to work when organisms reproduce. Therefore, the change of the automobile over time is not comparable.

3. This seems reasonable and reflects a legitimate slippery slope. Note that the argument has anticipated one of the factors that might prevent the slippery slope — namely, teaching to the contrary. But in fact, people tend to act on their beliefs. Therefore, the belief that a person is a mere animal will tend to result in comparable behavior.

4. This seems reasonable and is not a fallacy. Since solar panels provide free energy without pollution, the stated outcome is likely.

5. This is a false analogy because we have good reasons to believe in God, but children do not have good reasons to believe in the tooth fairy. The beliefs are not similar, because one is justified

and the other is not.

6. This is a false analogy for two reasons. First, an accurate clock is set to the current time when it is activated, whereas radioactive elements are not. Second, a clock tells us the current time, not the age of the clock, whereas radiometric dating is supposed to discover the age of the rock.

7. This is a false analogy, and a rather subtle one. There is a similarity between humans developing from a single fertilized cell, and the idea that humans evolved from a single-celled organism. But this similarity is only superficial, because the two cells under consideration are very different. A human fertilized cell (a zygote) is human already, has human DNA, and all the instructions in that DNA to code for all the traits that a human has. However, the first cell from which all life supposedly evolved is not human, does not have human DNA, and lacks the instructions in the DNA that would code for all the traits that a human has. The analogy is falsely comparing a human becoming a human, with a single-celled micro-organism becoming a human.

8. This is a fitting analogy. The two (very different) things are compared in ways in which they are genuinely similar. Namely, a joke ceases to be funny (its purpose) when "dissected" just as a frog ceases to live (its purpose) when dissected. This is a poetic use of analogy, which is appropriate.

9. This is a slippery slope fallacy. Long before the house became "full of dogs," a family would likely stop adopting new ones.

10. This is a false analogy because there is no relevant similarity between the two concepts.

Chapter 29: Review of the Fallacies of Presumption

1. This is a question-begging epithet. No argument has been presented. The person simply uses biased language to assert his case. He claims that evidence supports his position, but he doesn't actually provide a single example.

2. This is a hasty generalization. The earth is only one example, and it happens to be the exceptional case. The proper procedure would be to sample thousands of planets. Extrapolating from just one example is always a hasty generalization fallacy.

3. This is special pleading. Evolution is also not observable or testable in the present. Yet, the arguer considers it to be scientific. He is exempting his

own position from the criteria used to dismiss the creation position. He is using a double standard.

4. This is the no true Scotsman fallacy and possibly also special pleading. The term "real" implies that creationist journals do not count, thereby defining "journal" in a biased way — the no true Scotsman fallacy. Moreover, if he is going to insist that the creationist use only journals opposite to the creationist's position, then why will he not abide by that standard, too? To be fair, we could ask the evolutionist to use only creationist journals to make his argument, not evolutionist ones. He has exempted himself from his own standard — special pleading.

5. This is the fallacy of false analogy. Gravity is observable, testable, and repeatable in the present, unlike particles-to-people evolution.

6. This is a sweeping generalization fallacy. Most people don't come back to life (not yet anyway). So the generalization is true. But that doesn't mean that there are no exceptions. God can indeed raise the dead and has done so.

7. This is the fallacy of false cause — specifically the *post hoc ergo propter hoc*. That the lower test scores happened after the event does not mean that they were caused by the event. The argument fails to provide any evidence that the succession is necessary.

8. This is a bifurcation fallacy. We are presented with only two options, neither of which is correct. The third unstated (correct) option is that birds were created as birds.

9. This is a slippery slope fallacy. Since miracles (whether they involve a temporary suspension of the laws of nature or not) are rare by definition, we could easily distinguish a miracle from the normal flow of nature. Thus, science would not come to a halt.

10. This is the fallacy of begging the question. Since the way we got here is the very claim at issue, the arguer has merely assumed what he is attempting to prove.

Chapter 30: *Ad Hominem*

1. This is a classic example of the abusive *ad hominem*. All examples of name-calling are *ad hominem* fallacies, and utterly irrelevant to the truth of an argument.

2. This is not a fallacy. We are evaluating the claims of

a witness, not an argument. And it is reasonable to be skeptical about the claims of a notorious liar.

3. This is an abusive *ad hominem*. The critic objects to something about the person making an argument, rather than attempting to refute the actual argument.

4. This is a classic example of the circumstantial *ad hominem*. Notice that the arguer is confusing causes with reasons. The cause of belief in creation may indeed be my Christian upbringing. But my reasons for believing in creation are many (it is recorded history in the Bible, it is confirmed by scientific evidence, etc.). The arguer is pointing that the person is motivated to argue in a particular way due to his circumstances: hence, the circumstantial *ad hominem*.

5. This is *ad hominem* because the argument is dismissed because the person who (originally) made it is objectionable. Hence, this is an abusive *ad hominem*. But no rational argument against the original claim has been made.

6. There is no fallacy here. The claim that the records are inaccurate might need to be further supported, but it is entirely reasonable to conclude that someone might draw false conclusions on the basis of inaccurate data.

7. This is the circumstantial *ad hominem* fallacy. The motivations for making an argument are irrelevant to the cogency of the argument.

8. This is a circumstantial *ad hominem* argument. The atheist is assuming that the theist is motivated to believe in God for psychological reasons — because of his circumstances. Whether that is so is entirely irrelevant to God's existence or to the person's argument for God's existence. Remember, the motivation for making an argument is irrelevant to its cogency or lack thereof.

9. This is an abusive *ad hominem* fallacy. This type of argument occurs when the person cannot make a rational case, and therefore attacks the person: calling him a racist or some other derogatory term.

10. This is an *ad hominem* fallacy because it is directed against the person, rather than his argument as presented in his research. I suggest it is in the abusive category because it questions Dr. Johnston's competence due to lack of experience. But this is utterly irrelevant to any arguments made in his research. Such arguments should be evaluated on their own merit.

Chapter 31: The Faulty Appeal to Authority

1. This is the faulty appeal to authority. It fails in at least the first and second way, and possibly the third as well. Namely, evolution is a belief about how life came about in the past, but only a small fraction of evolutionists are qualified historians; further, even historian evolutionists do not believe in evolution on the basis of historical documents. Second, and most importantly, many scientists have a naturalistic worldview, which causes them to reject biblical creation at the outset. Third, the majority of scientists are fallible, even when they research correctly in their area. (By the way, the answer to the original [rhetorical] question is: sin.)

2. This is a faulty appeal to authority. Most biology textbooks are written be people with a fallacious, unbiblical worldview which will affect how they interpret the data. So, this fails in at least way #2. Furthermore, biology is the study of life in the present world; biologists are not qualified to say what supposedly happened millions of years ago. So it fails in way #1 as well.

3. This is the faulty appeal to authority. It seems to fail in all three ways. No Ph.D. or M.D. has actual experience in what happened millions of years ago. No one has. Many Ph.D. and M.D.s are creationists, so this fails in the second way. And the dogmatism with which the person asserts that evolution is clearly true suggests that he is treating this expert as infallible — way #3.

4. This is a faulty appeal to authority. It fails in at least the first and second way. Science does not qualify someone to say on his own authority what happened in the distant past. And there is a strong minority of scientists who do not believe in millions of years. So worldview considerations are at issue.

5. The is a faulty appeal to authority in at least way #1 and #2. The reasons are the same as the previous question.

6. This is a faulty appeal to authority in way #1 and #2. I trust what physicists say about gravity and electricity because they have education and experience in these issues. They do not have experience in what supposedly happened in the distant past (creation or evolution). They are not qualified on that issue. Second, creationists and evolutionists have different worldviews, but basically agree on gravity, electricity, chemistry, etc. But our creation scientists do not accept evolution

in the Darwinian sense.

7. This is a faulty appeal to authority in at least way #1 and #2. Jim may be smart, but he has no experience of the distant past such that he could have observed the origin of life. Second, his worldview has not been considered. After all, there are smart people who believe in creation.

8. There is no fallacy. This passes tests #1, #2, and #3. God is knowledgeable of the origin of the universe because He was there, actually created it, and knows everything. God has a correct worldview because His thinking determines truth. And God is infallible. An unbeliever might want us to back up the claim that scripture is God's Word, and we will have to answer that. But there is no fallacy here.

9. This is a faulty appeal to authority in way #2. Bible scholars are certainly qualified to analyze the meaning of Scripture — so they pass #1. But they are not without biases. And many Bible scholars (such as Dr. Ken Gentry, or Dr. Steven Boyd) say that the days of Genesis cannot be long periods of time, but are in fact ordinary days. So this appeal fails to pass criterion #2.

10. This is not a fallacy, because the Bible is God's Word, and God (1) is an expert on everything, (2) has a correct worldview and always interprets evidence correctly, and (3) is infallible. Again, the unbeliever will want to know how we know that the Bible is God's Word, and we can readily accommodate him. But an appeal to Scripture is never fallacious.

Chapter 32: The Strawman Fallacy

1. Lots of possible answers here. Basically, any claim that the Bible says something that it does not actually say, or that Christians believe things that we really don't. "Christians don't believe in science because they have blind faith." "The Bible claims that dinosaurs never existed, but clearly they did."

2. It is immoral because it is a lie. It is bearing false witness against your neighbor to claim that he believes something that he doesn't actually believe.

3. Lots of possible answers here, because there are many possibilities. Evolutionists have tried to link science with evolution to the extent that denying one is said to be like denying the other. Their propaganda campaign has been quite successful. Alternatively, some creationists (unfortunately) really do deny science, albeit somewhat

inconsistently. An evolutionist might take these few examples as falsely representing creationists in general — the hasty generalization fallacy.

4. The key is to carefully study the position that we are refuting, do not take shortcuts by making assumptions, and represent that position (no matter how absurd) as fairly as we can. This might entail asking our opponents to clarify what they believe about certain things. (Knowledge of the position is the essential necessity.)

5. [Many answers are possible.] We need to educate unbelievers in what it is that Christianity actually entails. When people misrepresent the Christian position, we should correct them with gentleness and respect so that the error is not propagated further. We should do our best to represent opposing positions accurately as an example for others.

Chapter 33: Faulty Appeals

1. This is the appeal to ignorance. The lack of proof against the Oort cloud does not prove the existence of the Oort cloud.

2. Appeal to fear/force. The threat of being fired is used to coerce a belief that is (potentially) logically unsupported.

3. Appeal to pity. The person is attempting to appeal to our sense of pity to coerce agreement with him on a position that has not been logically demonstrated.

4. Appeal to emotion. The person attempts to capitalize on our sense of patriotism and love for freedom and democracy to support a position that has not been demonstrated by logical means. (This would not be a fallacy if it occurred at the end of a speech where the person had already demonstrated logically that Republicans better represent America/freedom/democracy than their competitors. But, in isolation, it is fallacious.)

5. Appeal to emotion. The vocation and facilities of the authors has no bearing whatsoever on their argument. The person attempts to stir emotion rather than making a logical argument.

6. Appeal to ignorance. The (alleged) lack of proof against evolution is not the same as positive evidence in favor of evolution.

7. Appeal to pity. Teachers face this fallacy all the time. The student attempts to persuade the teacher of something false by inciting feelings of sympathy. But the consequences of the student failing the class has

no logical bearing on the appropriate grade.

8. Appeal to ignorance. The lack of evidence against other universes is not the same as positive evidence for other universes. We could equally well argue that "there must not be other universes because no one has proved that they exist."

9. Appeal to emotion. The person attempts to tap into our disgust for Hitler, and transfer that to the position he is against.

10. Not a fallacy. Repeated success is good evidence for a particular law of nature.

Chapter 34: Naturalistic, Moralistic, and the Appeal to Consequences

1. This is the appeal to consequences fallacy. The fact that it is undesirable that some people end up in hell does not affect the fact that they do.

2. This is the naturalistic fallacy because it draws a conclusion about morality based on what happens. But not everything that happens is morally commendable.

3. This is not a fallacy. The conclusion is a factual claim based on an appeal to authority. However, the appeal to authority is not faulty since doctors are experts in the cause of disease.

4. This is not a fallacy. The conclusion is a moral one based on the moral teachings of the Bible. Since God disapproves of what is wrong, and since the Bible tells us that lying is something God disapproves of, the conclusion follows necessarily.

5. This is the moralistic fallacy. The conclusion is about what is supposedly true (scientists do not falsify data), but it is based solely on the fact that falsifying data would be morally wrong. But scientists do not always act morally. So the conclusion does not follow.

6. This is a classic example of the fallacy of the appeal to consequences. It may be undesirable that animals less fit to their environment are more likely to die. But that doesn't change the reality that they are.

7. This is the naturalistic fallacy. The fact that many people do something has no bearing on whether the act in question is morally commendable.

8. This is an appeal to consequences fallacy. The fact that it is horrible that Hitler slaughtered Jews does not change the fact that he did.

9. This is the moralistic fallacy. The arguer has

fallaciously made a claim about reality merely based on what is morally appropriate. But in reality, people sometimes behave immorally.

10. This is the naturalistic fallacy. The arguer fallaciously concludes that since something is a particular way (namely a law against murder helps people survive) that something is morally right. But just because a law against murder indeed helps a society to thrive does not make it morally right. Hypothetically, a civil law that required all people to reproduce at least 5 children would cause society to expand and grow, but it would be an immoral law because it is contrary to God's approval.

Chapter 35: The Genetic Fallacy and the *Tu Quoque* Fallacy

1. *Tu quoque* fallacy. The fact that the opponent may also be guilty of mishandling money does not refute the claim that the first candidate is also mishandling money.

2. Genetic fallacy. The source in question has not been demonstrated to be unreliable. Hence, to dismiss its claims is arbitrary and irrational. Furthermore, the occupation of the authors of a book are irrelevant to the cogency of any arguments in the book.

3. Genetic fallacy. The origin of an idea is not relevant to the truth of the idea. Of course, the arguer is merely stating a conjecture about the origin of an idea, not its actual historically documented origin. Namely, belief in God did not originate as he suggests. Rather, belief in God existed from the beginning since God revealed Himself to Adam and Eve.

4. *Tu quoque* fallacy. The claim that the environmentalists may fail to apply their own teaching and would thus be hypocrites is utterly irrelevant to the cogency of their arguments in favor of caring for our environment.

5. *Tu quoque* fallacy. Yes, the police officer may have been speeding too, but this does not absolve the civilian of his crime. Moreover, the law exempts police officers from speed limits under these conditions.

6. Not a fallacy. The *National Enquirer* is established to be unreliable, and therefore it is appropriate to be skeptical of claims made in its pages, unless they can be verified by a more reliable source.

7. *Tu quoque* fallacy. Some professing Christians are

indeed hypocrites. But this is utterly irrelevant to the truth of the Christian worldview.

8. Genetic fallacy. Information scientists present arguments in favor of certain truth claims. Their arguments stand or fall on their own merit. The worldview of the scientists is irrelevant to the cogency of their arguments / demonstrations.

Chapter 36: The Fallacy of Irrelevant Thesis

1. This is the fallacy of irrelevant thesis (and might also be considered a circumstantial *ad hominem*) because whether a person is a Christian is not relevant to the truth of origins.

2. This is not a fallacy. The evolutionist's claim is wrong, but it is not an error in reasoning. His claim is very relevant to the creationist's question.

3. This is the fallacy of irrelevant thesis. Jimmy's statement may well be true, but it is not relevant to the fact that he cheated on the exam and has no excuse for it.

4. This is the fallacy of irrelevant thesis. Without any further explanation, there appears to be no rational connection between Dad's statement (which may well be true) and Timothy's question.

5. This is the fallacy of irrelevant thesis. Ordinary days are caused by the rotation of earth relative to a light source. This has been true since the first day of creation where God created the light in verse 3 and we see that the earth was already rotating and had evening and morning in verse 5. The fact that God used a temporary light source for the first three days before replacing it with the sun on day four is utterly irrelevant to the definition of "day."

6. This it the fallacy of irrelevant thesis. The claim is not that a professed atheist cannot have a sense of morality and act morally at times. Rather, the claim is that the atheist cannot justify morality on his own worldview. So his response is utterly irrelevant to the claim at issue. (This particular error occurs often in debates.)

7. This is a reasonable inference, not a fallacy. The person's answer to the question is relevant to the question. And it is a reasonable answer, though not conclusive.

8. This is a classic example of the fallacy of irrelevant thesis. It is quite true that if animals didn't have parts that worked together then they would have died. However, this is utterly irrelevant to the question at issue: why? The answer to that question

is "because they were designed by the mind of God." Evolutionists often use this fallacious answer to distract from the fact that they cannot cogently answer the question at issue with their own worldview.

9. This is a fallacy of irrelevant thesis because the premise that "this will not solve all the world's problems" may be true but is irrelevant to the conclusion that "people who want to reduce the number of guns in the world are mistaken." Perhaps those people are indeed mistaken. But the reason given does not support the conclusion and is in fact irrelevant to it.

10. There is no fallacy here. The reason given is relevant. It may require more explanation, but it is relevant.

Chapter 37: Review of Fallacies of Relevance

1. This is the genetic fallacy. An argument should be evaluated on its merit, not its source.

2. This is the fallacy of irrelevant thesis. The question at issue is not whether the atheist can use laws of logic. Rather, the claim is that the atheist cannot account for laws of logic — make sense of them within his own professed worldview. The atheist has answered the wrong question.

3. This is the appeal to force/fear. That legal action might result is irrelevant to the truth of creation.

4. This is the naturalistic fallacy. Just because something *is* a particular way does not mean that it *should be* that way. The fact that many people abort babies does not make it right.

5. This is the faulty appeal to authority/majority. People have a sin nature and, as such, do not always draw the most reasonable conclusion given the data.

6. This is the circumstantial *ad hominem* fallacy. The fact that Dr. Dave is motivated to make an argument does not mean that his argument is unsound.

7. This is the fallacy of irrelevant thesis. Whether or not creation is classified as "science" is totally irrelevant to whether or not it is true.

8. This is the appeal to ignorance. Such a fallacy is always reversible. We could respond, "Well, then there must not be an Oort cloud; no one has any proof that it does exist."

9. This is an abusive *ad hominem* fallacy. The person

attempts to refute an argument by attacking the intelligence of the person rather than dealing with the facts of the argument.

10. This is a strawman fallacy because it misrepresents the creationist position. Creationists do believe in the scientific method. In fact, only the Bible can account for science since science is based on induction.

Quiz Answers

Quiz #1 — chapters 1–9

1. Logic
2. illogical
3. rational
4. reason
5. character
6. proposition
7. argument
8. premises
9. negation
10. Faith

Quiz #2 — chapters 10–14

1. arbitrary
2. lexical
3. precising
4. syllogism
5. fallacy
6. Premise: *The Bible tells you to go to church. (Note the premise indicator word "since.")*

    Conclusion: *You really should go to church.*
7. Premise: *Murder violates God's law. (Note the premise indicator word "because.")*

    Conclusions: *We shouldn't murder.*
8. Unstated premise: *All Celtics are basketball players.*
9. Unstated conclusion: *Therefore, Socrates is mortal.*
10. Unstated major premise: *"That which is non-literal is not really real"* or *"That which does not literally select anything is not really real."*

Quiz #3 — chapters 15–19

1. Reification fallacy. Science here is personified as if it can say something, and is used to draw a conclusion.
2. Equivocation fallacy. The argument invokes evolution in the generic sense of change to prove neo-Darwinian evolution, which is quite different.
3. Fallacy of accent. Courtney misunderstood Emily by placing the emphasis on the word "Brent" rather than the word "didn't."
4. Equivocation fallacy. The argument attempts to prove evolution in the neo-Darwinian sense by giving examples of other types of change, which are irrelevant to Darwinian evolution.
5. Fallacy of composition. Though the human body is made of parts that have no free will, it does not follow that humans have no free will.
6. Fallacy of division. Just because the brain has consciousness does not mean that the parts of the brain have parts of consciousness.
7. Fallacy of composition. Only one person can win a race.
8. Equivocation fallacy. The changes observed within bacteria are "evolution" of a sort, but do not establish evolution in the particles-to-people sense.
9. Fallacy of accent. Samantha has placed undue emphasis on the "s" in girls, thereby changing the meaning.
10. Reification fallacy. Time is treated as if it is a conscious, thinking person and is used as part of an argument against God.

Quiz #4 — chapters 20–30

1. False cause fallacy — the *cum hoc ergo propter hoc.* The unproven assumption is that atheism has caused the crime rates to be lower, merely on the basis that they go together.
2. Bifurcation fallacy. The consistent Christian believes in creation and the methods of science.
3. Question-begging epithet. Loaded language is used to persuade, not a rational argument.
4. No true Scotsman fallacy. The word "real" is prefixed to science to redefine the term such that hypotheses must be restricted to natural explanations. However, the definition of science only requires testability, not *natural* explanations.
5. Fallacy of complex question. The question should be divided: "Is there evidence for an old earth?" And, "If so, how can that be if Genesis is true?" Since the answer to the first question is "no," the second question is unnecessary.
6. Begging the question. The way life came about is the very question at issue. The argument arbitrarily assumes evolution as the proof of evolution.

7. Sweeping generalization fallacy. Generally, it is impossible for the dead to be raised. Jesus is an exception because He is God.

8. Fallacy of false analogy. Gravity is testable and repeatable in the present, but particles-to-people evolution is not.

9. Hasty generalization fallacy. The earth is an infinitesimal part of the universe. Hence, experiences on earth are insufficient to extrapolate what happens in the rest of the universe.

10. Slippery slope fallacy. The action is not likely to set off such a chain of events.

Quiz #5 — chapters 31–38

1. Appeal to consequences fallacy. That something would be nice doesn't make it true.

2. Faulty appeal to authority. That scientists and theologians think that evolution may be compatible with God is irrelevant to whether evolution is actually compatible with God. An appeal to authority has replaced logical argumentation.

3. Fallacy of irrelevant thesis. That God does or allows things that some people don't like is utterly irrelevant to the issue of God's existence.

4. Appeal to fear/force. Rather than making a rational argument against creation, the threat of legal action is used to persuade.

5. Naturalistic fallacy. What people actually do is not relevant to what people should or should not do.

6. Strawman fallacy. That creationists reject scientific facts or evidence is simply false and misrepresents the creationist position.

7. Appeal to emotion. The statements are intended to stir emotions of appreciation for nature, rather than making a rational argument for evolution.

8. Appeal to pity. We are supposed to feel sorry for those poor teachers who want to enlighten their students about the truth of evolution, but cannot do so due to legal/political pressure. But no argument for evolution has been made.

9. *Tu quoque* fallacy. The apparent hypocrisy of the environmentalists does not disprove their argument.

10. Moralistic fallacy. The argument assumes that something does not happen on the basis that it would be unethical.

Final Exam Answers

. Moralistic fallacy. The argument assumes that something does not happen on the basis that it would be unethical.

2. No true Scotsman fallacy. The implication is that creationist journals are not "real," yet this goes beyond the dictionary definition of a journal.

3. Fallacy of complex question. It should be divided into "Do you deny science?" And, "If so, then why?"

4. Faulty appeal to authority. The "scientific community" is invoked as if it were an infallible authority — the standard for all truth claims.

5. Fallacy of division. The soul does not divide into the parts of the body.

6. Begging the question. The way life came about is the very question at issue. The argument arbitrarily assumes evolution as the proof of evolution.

7. Bifurcation fallacy. The Christian position is that we should use our brain to reason from what the Bible says.

8. *Tu quoque* fallacy. The apparent hypocrisy of the environmentalists does not disprove their argument.

9. Fallacy of composition. Though the human body is made of parts that have no free will, it does not follow that humans have no free will.

10. False cause fallacy. That nearly all mammals have seven vertebrae in their neck does not establish that the cause is evolution from a common ancestor.

11. Naturalistic fallacy. What happens in nature does not establish what is morally right. Some animals eat their own young, but obviously this is not right for people.

12. Fallacy of irrelevant thesis. The persuasiveness of an argument does not establish (and is irrelevant to) the soundness of an argument.

13. Special pleading. Evolutionists *also* have an explanation that they are unwilling to alter — that natural forces alone are responsible for the universe and life. They have arbitrarily exempted themselves from their own standard.

14. Faulty appeal to authority. That scientists and theologians think that evolution may be compatible with God is irrelevant to whether evolution is actually compatible with God. An appeal to authority has replaced logical argumentation.

15. Question-begging epithet. A proper comparison would be evolution vs. creation — not creationism. By adding the "ism," the argument implies that creation is merely a belief and that evolution is not, but without making any argument for it. Loaded language is no substitute for logic.

16. Sweeping generalization fallacy. Generally, it is impossible for the dead to be raised. Jesus is an exception because He is God.

17. Reification fallacy. Plants and animals are personified as if part of an army that can "invade." The reification is a fallacy if the statement is part of an argument.

18. Fallacy of accent. Courtney misunderstood Emily by placing the emphasis on the word "Brent" rather than the word "didn't."

19. Strawman fallacy. That creationists reject scientific facts or evidence is simply false and misrepresents the creationist position.

20. Appeal to consequences fallacy. That something would be nice doesn't make it true.